Billy the Blackfella from Bourke

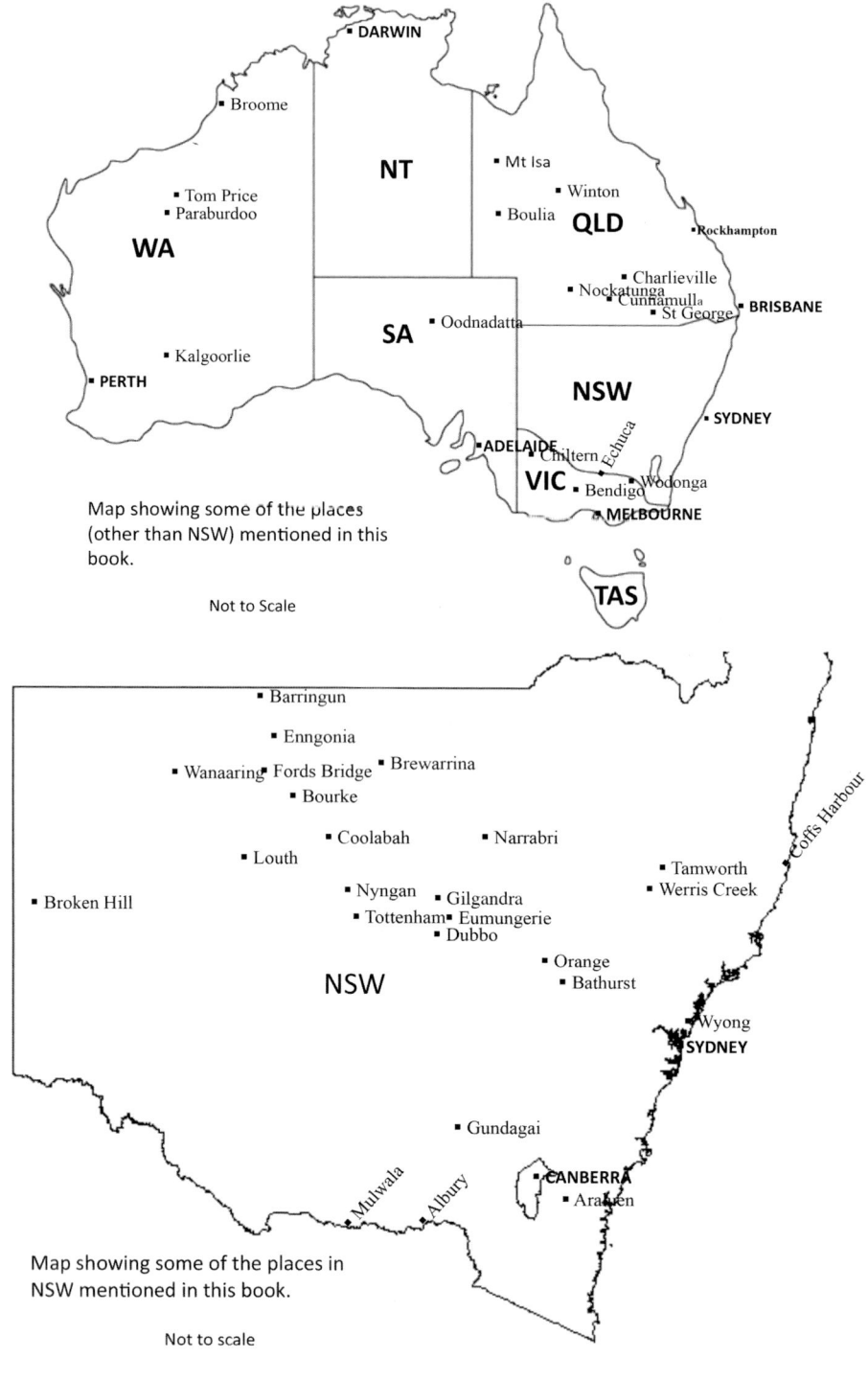

Billy the Blackfella from Bourke

Edited and transcribed by Chris Woodland

Map of part of South America showing places mentioned in this book.

Not to scale

ROSENBERG

First published in Australia in 2015
by Rosenberg Publishing Pty Ltd
PO Box 6125, Dural Delivery Centre NSW 2158
Phone: 61 2 9654 1502 Fax: 61 2 9654 1338
Email: rosenbergpub@smartchat.net.au
Web: www.rosenbergpub.com.au

Copyright © Chris Woodland 2015

All rights reserved. No part of this publication may be reproduced, stored in a retrieval system, or transmitted, in any form or by any means, electronic, mechanical, photocopying, recording or otherwise, without the prior permission of the publisher in writing.

National Library of Australia Cataloguing-in-Publication entry

Creator: Woodward, Chris, author.

Title: Billy the blackfella from Bourke / Chris Woodward.

ISBN: 9781925078688 (paperback)
ISBN: 9781925078695 (ebook)
ISBN: 9781925078824 (epdf)

Notes: Includes index.

Subjects: Gray, Bill, 1940-2011.
Aboriginal Australians–New South Wales–Bourke–Biography.
Drovers–Australia–Biography.
Oil industry workers–South America-Biography.
Well drillers–South America–Biography.
Bourke (N.S.W.)–History.

Dewey Number: 305.89915092

Printed in China by Prolong Press Limited

Contents

Introduction   7
Acknowledgements   13
Part One   15
  Bourke – the Early Days   15
  School Days   20
  Life on the Reserve   22
  Gypsies and Afghans   26
  The Public School   28
  Enngonia and Station Work   30
  Droving and Photo of Mother   35
  Learning to Ride   37
  Argument and Family Deaths   39
  Droving and Strange Things in the Night   42
  Injury, Swearing and Tucker from the River   45
  Personalities and Old Customs   49
  Colourful Days at Enngonia Reserve   59
  Visit to Sydney, Araluen and Nerrigundah   67
  Splinter Reynolds and Bert 'Murri' Powell   70
  Marriage   75
  Billy Joins Forces with the Police and Revisits Sydney   79
  The Cuffes of New Park   82
  Life after New Park   84
  Moves to Rockhampton and Becomes a Part-Time Entertainer   87
  To Brisbane   90
  Central New South Wales and Romance   94
  Drilling in Western Australia   97

Part Two   101
   South America – Ecuador   101
   R&R in Manta – Discrimination – Student Sex Workers   110
   Colombia to Venezuela – Corruption   113
   Maracaibo and Cartagena   119
   Caqueta and Casual 'Wives'   122
   Home and Family   125
   Singapore and Indonesia   127
   Dubious Dealings   132

Part Three   135
   Home to Stay – Business Venture   135
   Back to Bourke   139
   Kalgoorlie – Orange – Heart Attack   141
   Driving a Bus in Bathurst   144
   Having a Go – Discrimination – Acceptance   146

Part Four   150
   Beyond Oodnadatta – Desert People   150
   Memorable Anecdotes   152
   Family Secrets   156
   Bush Tucker and Leaf Players   159
   Postscript   161

Index   166

Introduction

The popular saying that everyone has a story to tell is very true. Every person leads an interesting life reasonably different to others'. Billy Gray, the subject of this book, was perhaps noticeably different to most others. His story is one of having been born in an era before his people were considered to be Australian citizens, though some of his ancestors had been resident in this continent before Europe was peopled by modern man; he was a man of limited formal education yet he visited isolated areas of the world, not as a tourist, but as a worker. He had been brought up to know his place: that he was a second-class person, who must remain in the background. In South America he found for the first time in his life that he could move freely without experiencing that feeling of being an outcast; he just blended in.

It was January 1959 and very hot when I first met Billy Gray on New Park station. The property extends from the Bourke to Cunnamulla road in Queensland, and runs east along the border on the Queensland side for about 32 kilometres. Though we had a lot in common, no one would have thought that it was the beginning of a close relationship that lasted for 52 years. As young men we both loved singing around the campfire at night, enjoyed tracking down and shooting wild pigs, and had an earnest interest in the bush, its history, what grew in it, the creatures that inhabited it, the tales of the old people about the early days, the drovers and the outback people generally, particularly the original inhabitants. The Aboriginal side of Billy's heredity represented the longest continued culture on earth.

Chris Woodland and Billy Gray, New Park station, Barringun, 1959

My interest in the First Australians began when I was an infant at Kempsey on the mid-north coast of New South Wales. No doubt my tolerant and humanitarian parents had a lot to do with my attitude and subsequent fondness for this subject. The first Aboriginal family I was associated with were the Mumblers, who, like many others, came in from Burnt Bridge reserve to do whatever work they could find around the town. My parents had a strong sense of natural justice and were appalled that old Mr Mumbler, who had worked as a police tracker, did not receive a pension when he was retired. Our neighbours across the road in Austral Street would give their indigenous house cleaner all their old clothes, then deduct the value from their paltry earnings.

Later, almost at the age of fifteen, I experienced what was probably the most adventurous episode of my lifetime. My uncle, who had been a Native Affairs officer on Melville Island with the Tiwi people, made it all possible. Following his time on Melville Island, Kevin Woodland had been moved to Darwin. After visiting Sydney he drove my brother and me in his 1940 Buick up to Darwin over roads that would be unimaginable to those of later generations. The lack of decent roads and signposts, the drovers' breaks and campfire spotted stock routes, the batwing doors on the outback pubs, the burnt black spots on the bar fronts where the drovers and ringers had positively extinguished their cigarette butts, and all the abandoned army vehicles alongside the welcome bituminised Stuart Highway in the Northern Territory were of another world. It was late 1952 and Darwin Harbour was scattered with bombed ships, the legacy of a war that had finished seven years previously. A few years later the Japanese bought all the wrecks and shipped the scrap iron back to their resource-poor country. In Darwin I met Moreen (also known as Ginger One and Matthias Ulungura) the first Australian to capture a Japanese on Australian soil. This occurred when the Japanese pilot crashed on Melville Island.

Though Kevin was no longer stationed on the island he had organised for my brother and me to stay with his friend Tom Carroll, his wife and young daughter. They were the only white people on the island.

To a 'bush mad' teenager my stay at Snake Bay was beyond my wildest dreams. I would never equal the experiences with tribal people again. It did nothing to allay my interest in the First Australians. Rather, that interest was intensified.

In 1959 Billy was a very handsome, lean and fit young man. His dark hair had a copper tinge to it and he wore a friendly smile showing a good set of teeth.

Each morning before breakfast he would run in the milking cow for the homestead on New Park. The horse paddock was much larger than the 50-acre dairy farm where I spent some of my childhood. Billy had no horse for this and he tracked the milker down through the budda bush and mulga scrub, then ran it back to the yard in his high-heeled riding boots.

Each night around the campfire Billy would play the guitar and sing. I would always sing along and sometimes contribute with the mouth organ. The songs we sang, such as Slim Dusty's 'The Rain Tumbles Down in July' and 'When the Sun Goes Down Outback', related to our own experiences. American Country and Western music was popular also, particularly songs by the well-liked Hank Williams. Later in life Billy became aware of, and besotted with, the Afro-American country music performers such as Charley Pride. It was Billy who taught me my first three guitar chords.

Yarns were also common around the campfire. Billy was an interesting raconteur. His tales, including the one of a heavily pregnant Aboriginal woman having to clamber up on the back of a mail truck while young white men enjoyed seats in the driver's cabin, and stories of the ways and customs of the Old People, always intrigued me.

Music was always an important part of Billy's life. Later in Queensland he became involved with a band performing in pubs. First they got Billy up to sing. Then later he also accompanied the group by playing the bass guitar. In his later life it was sad to see him unable to play the guitar, as his hands would not respond because of the hard work they'd endured. By then he relied on cassettes tapes, and then CDs, to address that essential part of his life.

Billy had a strong work ethic, a trait he learnt from his foster-father Alf Hagan. Never afraid of hard work, Billy worked at many occupations. He was experienced in working stock on sheep and cattle stations, droving, fencing, taxi driving, as a factory labourer, water and oil driller and more. He worked in many parts of Australia and various parts of South America and Indonesia. His travels and experiences gave him a deep understanding of the cultures of different peoples.

Though Billy and I kept in contact over the years there were times when we did lose touch with each other. We discovered later that when he was water drilling in the Mulwala/Yarrawonga area along the Murray River, my family and I were living about 600 metres away in a straight line from the hotel where he was staying.

In writing this account of Billy Gray's life I discovered I had two choices: to write from my experiences and knowledge of the man, or let him tell his story in his own words, the latter being the more difficult of the two. I decided to let him express the story in his own way.

It would be appropriate to mention that Billy was actually given the name William at birth. Commonly, many Williams become known as Bill, of which Billy is an extension, particularly when the person is younger, and it is more than a usual practice with Aboriginal people. As Billy grew older he liked to be introduced as Bill, but to his family and friends he was always Billy, or Uncle Billy to his nephews and nieces.

I recorded Billy's story in the last few days of 1991 with a tape-recorder on loan from the Oral History Section of the National Library of Australia. These tapings are the basis of this book. It was the more difficult path to go down, as a writer/editor has to maintain the integrity of such an oral history. All people speak differently to the way they would write and the same people do not always speak in the same manner at all times, as they articulate more naturally as they relax and they will use expressions more natural to them.

The eminent English linguist David Crystal says that spoken English – in this case Australian English – is different from written English and the difference is much greater than people imagine. There are many reasons for this variation other than an interviewee instinctively altering his speech at the sight of a microphone. Hesitation in talking is more pronounced and yet speakers continue their conversation without awareness of punctuation. They do not have to worry about their pauses, lapses and change of direction. In writing from the oral, or transcribed oral source, in many instances it is difficult to decide when one sentence finishes and another commences.

I have refrained from altering the meaning of Billy's story, but have had to edit often because of the problems mentioned. However, at no time have

I found it necessary to alter the context of Billy's remarkable story and I have maintained the integrity of his interview. As stated earlier, people speak differently at different times, and over the five days that I recorded Billy, this did occur. Mostly when talking to me in a more relaxed state Billy would, like many people, say *me* instead of *my*. Generally I have used the latter in this text, though he used *me* considerably during the interview. When more at ease he would use the term *blackfellas*. Occasionally he would be more formal and say blackfellows

Unfortunately just a few spellings of placenames and the names of people may be incorrect. Despite much time seeking out the correct spelling for these terms, a few are dubious.

Certain topics were discussed several times over the five days and mostly it was sensible to organise them together for the sake of the reader.

Because of the above, Billy's personal voice, with its distinctive intonations and accent, cannot be fully appreciated. Of course a CD of one of his yarns would be an ideal complement to this publication.

Many people may find some of the terms used by Billy to be politically incorrect. Those expressions are still very much in use today among the Aboriginal people. Billy was proud to be a *blackfella* and he knew me as a *whitefella*. They were, and are, accepted lingo. Besides, we were beyond colour and the words were just that, words. The couple of times he called me a white Murri (white blackfella) made me feel honoured. On several occasions over many years, when Billy was happy with some achievement he would say, 'Not bad for an old blackfella from Bourke, eh?'

The interview with Billy can be accessed at the Oral History Section of the National Library of Australia under TRC 3002. A 1994 interview with Billy and his sister Joanie (TRC 3000/92), which was conducted by noted folklorist John Meredith and myself, can also be accessed.

Chris Woodland
Bawley Point, NSW
April 2015

Acknowledgements

Throughout the long gestation of this work I have enjoyed kind and generous assistance from many people. All have contributed to this book in their own particular way. Unfortunately, over time there must be names that I have overlooked, not because of the value of their input but because of my absentmindedness. I apologise for any such omission. My sincere thanks go to:

Billy's family, particularly his two sons Justin and Casey, both of Tamworth, and his sister Joanie of Mildura.

The late John Meredith who first implanted the idea of a book after reading the oral history interview in the late '90s. For John I belatedly thank him for that suggestion and the innumerable ideas he offered me throughout our long friendship.

My family, particularly my wife Virginia, continually supported my efforts, as did all members of the Woodland Clan, who all enjoyed the company and shared experiences with Billy. Virginia's computer knowledge greatly limited my use of insensitive words and frustrations while handling that recalcitrant machine.

The late Jim Kiley who was a poet and retired drover of Bourke. Jim contributed much to my passion for outback knowledge. He will always be remembered for his company, his songs and poetry.

David Billingham who kindly provided me with information on the Towri Aboriginal Corporation. Previous to David's assistance the term Towri was misunderstood during the transcription of Billy's interview.

Stephen Hagan, editor of the *National Indigenous Times* and distant relative of Billy Gray.

Mark Cranfield (past curator), Kevin Bradley (present curator), Shelley Grant and other helpful staff at the Oral History Section of the National Library of Australia, who have supported my collecting of oral history throughout the years. At all times I have found the Oral History Section of the NLA an area of efficient professionalism while possessing a helpful, friendly human environment.

Finally, author and oral historian Barry York, of Canberra, for giving me confidence in affirming that the project was worthwhile and should definitely be undertaken. Barry's friendship, editing, comments and suggestions have been invaluable.

PART ONE

To know Bourke is to know Australia

– Henry Lawson

Bourke – the Early Days

I was born in Bourke, New South Wales, in 1940, 15 June, 1940. I think my old auntie, the woman that reared me up, she got a bit muddled up in the date of birth, I think. I did not find out how old I was until I was about … I must have been about 24 or 25. I thought I was sort of 26, 27, but I was only 24, 25. I got my birth certificate.

Mum was a Knight. Her name was Jean Knight. She married a pommy bloke, an English bloke, George Gray, but … I never knew my mum. She died when I was very young and I was taken over by her sister, or half-sister, in Bourke, on the reserve.[1] We lived on the reserve in Bourke right up until 1948, I think it was. We moved up town, one of the first Aboriginal families to move up town from the reserve. We moved to Tudor Street; 26 Tudor Street, near the old coil factory.

[My mother] she committed suicide and then they thought she was murdered, poisoned; but I haven't found the truth. I mean, I've got to go back and go to the courthouse and see if I can dig up the case and have a read through it, just to see what actually happened.

A lot of things went on back in those days they [the Aboriginal people] didn't like talking about.

When he, my father, came to Bourke he was a station hand[2] and then he went on to the DMR [NSW Department of Main Roads] and he drove

---

1. The present Alice Edwards Village site.
2. A station hand was the common term for a multi-skilled person working on a rural property. The station hand's responsibilities could involve horse work, mustering, fencing, burr cutting, killing and butchering meat requirements for the homestead and employees' quarters, and many other tasks.

graders on the DMR for about 32 years. Then he transferred from Bourke to Wyong. That is back in the early '50s, about '52 or '53.

He never looked after us. When Mum died, my auntie took us, like Mum's half-sister, Janet Knight, and she married Alf Hagan. We were going to the home to be adopted out to different families, but they did not want to split us up. Alf Hagan married [during the war] Janet Knight and they took on three Cullen girls and me and my two sisters before they ever had any kids of their own. We lived at Toorale station for a long time there in our young days.

I'm not sure how old I was when my mother died, but Joanie tells me she can remember Mum.³ See, well, I can't, and there is a woman there somewhere in the back of my mind, but I just … I always thought it was Auntie Aggie but it could've been Mum. I might've been two year old, I don't know. But I don't sort of remember Mum's face and I was on the road droving with old Billy Howlett and we went out past Wanaaring and there was a woman there, Amy Johnson, old Duck Johnson and old Ruby's daughter, and we got talking about Mum. Auntie Betty was living at Wanaaring at the time and Ngaka was, I think he was dogging somewhere on a place somewhere up … ⁴

Billy's maternal grandmother, Lottie Bridge, was born at Deniliquin. A German-born policeman at Louth raped Lottie. Billy's mother, Jean, was the result of the assault.

That was in '57, '56, '57 … '57 I think it was, anyway she said, 'Don't you remember your mother?' this Amy Johnson, and I said, 'No, I didn't remember her,' so she said, 'Well I've got a photo over there, I'll go and get it.' And she brought the photo back and that was the first time I saw Mum,

---

3. Jean Gray died 19 January 1943, so Billy was almost two-and-a-half years of age.
4. Ngaka Ebsworth was working for the Wanaaring Pastoral Protection Board as a dogger, that is, a dingo trapper. Through marriage he was member of the extended Knight family. Ngaka is pronounced 'Knocker'.

Billy's mother, Jean Night, in Bourke's Central Park, 1930s.

This photo of Billy from 1943 appears to have been taken in Bourke at the Aboriginal camp by the Darling River.

Billy in 1947, probably at the family home in Tudor Street, Bourke, after the Hagan family had moved from the Aboriginal reserve.

Billy's sister, Joan, at 21 years of age, at 'The Rocks' (Aboriginal fish traps), Brewarrina, 1955.

in this photo. I've still got the photo, Amy gave it to me, I'll never forget her for that. First time I saw me mum's face and she's very, very much like Joanie. Very, very pretty; very much like her daughter.

Our father was going to let the government take us. We were going to be either in the Home or adopted out, probably to white people, I don't know. Anything could've happened to us back in those days but I can remember old George Gray sitting there with – he was nursing me – I was sitting on his knee and Joanie and Junie were standing there and we were all crying and I think that was about the time, and I can remember this woman leading me away and I don't know who it was. It was either … it might've been Mum I don't know, but I always thought it was Auntie Aggie, Aggie McKellar, because Junie … her mother and father had Junie when Junie was very small, and me and Joanie was more with Mum and Auntie Janet and her father and another bloke, 'Opie', Hope Alexander Knight. Opie was Mum's step-brother and Janet was her step-sister. Same mother and different father.

Mum's dad, as far as I can make out, was – I've asked a few old people about it – and they said he was a police sergeant in Louth. Albert Knight and Archie Knight, I had a yarn to them and I was trying to get a few stories out of them. The only thing they'd tell me about Mum was that her father was a police sergeant at Louth and that he was German. I'd like to know for sure.[5]

When Uncle Alf came back from the war in '45, he went to Toorale and he worked there as a station hand and he became head stockman. He was running some of the mustering camps before Toorale got cut up. It was a very big place and had about five or six mustering camps going at the one time and he was looking after them. I can remember Benny Wilson being in the camps there and an old bloke they used to call Doll Doll.[6] His right name was Charlie Marinor, but he got the name Doll Doll, his tribal name. He was a fullblood.

He was married, or lived with Ruby; Old Ruby Johnson. She had a lot of kids to Duck Johnson. He came from South Australia. A big, old man he was, with a big, bushy moustache and I can still remember him, actually. She had a

---

5. The old people said that this policeman had raped Lottie and that Jean was the result of that abuse.
6. Benny Wilson was a respected drover who was brought up on Winbar station near Louth on the Darling River. He eventually moved south and made his base at Hay on the Riverina.

wing of kids to him. Then they sort of split up and she got old Charlie Marinor. There are a few stories about them going around, but I wouldn't like to comment on them.

Gee, I wouldn't have a clue [from where Doll Doll originated from]. I know he was as black as the ace of spades and a very smart man.

Yes, well, he worked on Toorale for a long time. I can remember once in Bourke: there with old Doll Doll, we lined up when X-ray vans used to come around and have your chest X-rayed for TB and that, and he was in front of me. There was me and Archie Knight and Cook Ellwood and we were only big lumps of boys. Old Charlie was in front of us and the lady asked him – the nurse asked him – his name and he said, 'Charlie Marinor.' She said, 'How do you spell Marinor?' and he said, 'Bugger it, Doll Doll will do.' He couldn't read and write, you see.

School Days

I can remember my first day at school, Junie and Joanie and myself walking up to the convent school in Bourke. I started when I was just turned six, I think, and I saw my first sighting of the nuns in their black clothes and I thought they were ghosts and I was going to take off home. I went to school there for three years, the convent school. It was all right, but, you know, there was some of the white kids, some of them were good and some of them were sort of a bit racist.

I remember one bloke, Andrew Hill. He was a good mate of mine. We used to take johnnycake and corn meat and he used to like the johnnycake, so he used to swap us his nice sandwiches for our johnnycake, because he loved the johnnycake.[7]

We were living on the reserve then, on the town side of the river. I do not remember the other side of the river. I was very small, but a lot of my people lived on both sides of the river back in those days, and then we all finished up on one side, on the town side. Old grandfather, he bought a shop off Georgie Chinaman. That was Auntie Janet's father, George Knight. He bought the shop and we had that for a long time. Then Alf Hagan, he came back from the war and he won a bit of money on the racehorses and that is how we bought our house up town. We sold the shop to an old bloke called Fred Hull. Fred Hull, he was a white bloke. He used to live down the camp.

[The shop carried] just smallgoods, like mostly tinned meat and stuff, lollies and soft drinks, and I do not remember having ice-cream. I can remember my

---

7. A johnnycake is like a small damper, often cooked on the coals of a campfire or in a camp oven.

sister and I used to pinch the pink sticks off the shelf and then run outside and eat them and come back in and they would say, 'You've been pinching lollies!' We would say, 'No, no, we never pinched any lollies,' and you would poke your tongue out and of course, your tongue would be pink from eating pink [musk] sticks. You would get a slap under the ears for that.

I can remember once down the reserve, I think, before I started school. The old people used to settle their arguments with sticks, two sticks, and I saw this happen. I was on a swing that we had put up there and this Tommy Booth was a bit of a … he was a bit of a bully, you know. I was dressed for the pictures. We used to go up in the cart, the horse and cart, up town to the pictures. He pushed me off the swing and I got dirty and then I went bawling back over to Auntie Janet and told her and then the old grandfather got his sticks and went out and they had a few hits. Tommy Booth's father and old George Knight at it, because he was a bully who used to bully all the kids because he was a pretty big kid, Tommy Booth, but he is dead now, poor bugger.

That was years ago. Two sticks about two foot long and they knew how to use them, the old blokes. They just used fighting sticks; they wasn't shaped like a boondy. They just, you know, a piece off a tree, just a limb, but trimmed down to the right size and the right length. But sometimes they would do that. The older people used to do that, but the young ones used to knuckle up. They used to use the knuckle instead of the sticks.

Sometimes we would go to the pictures. They had the hall for the winter and the picture [theatre] – the old open air for the summer, side by side. The picture show was near the newsagents; Randall's. Old Mrs Randall used to own it, but they, all the blackfellas, when they went to the movies, they wasn't allowed back in the comfortable seats. They was all put down the front. Paid the same money.

That happened for a long time, but, old grandfather, when we moved up town, he walked in one night, paid at the door, bought the tickets and walked in and Junie and Joanie and myself was with him. He sat back sort of halfway and old Mrs Randall came down and put the torch on us and she said, 'Well, you can't sit here. You've got to go down the front.' He said, 'Well, I paid me money and it's the same as anybody else's, so I think I can sit here.' So anyway, they had a bit of an argument, but he refused to move anyway, the old bloke. So we ended up staying there. She was a bit racialist, old Mrs Randall.

Life on the Reserve

They were just old humpies on the reserve. I think the shop that the old Chinaman built was about the best house on the reserve then. It was built of corrugated iron with a cement floor. About the only place on the reserve that had a cement floor. All the rest of them were dirt.

Back in the '40s, they used to get a petrol ration in Bourke. They used to get petrol in four-gallon cans and when they used them they used to just throw them down the tip. The people used to go and get them and split them and they would finish up with a long piece of tin about three or four foot long and about eighteen inches wide, and that is what most of the camps were built with. They were, you know, a pretty good job. They done a pretty good job those old people.

Every house just about had a bough shed. Just a forky stick in the ground and a few rails on top. An old bloke there, old Rufus, I never knew his other name, he was a fullblood and he had an old T-model Ford. Most of the people outdoors had [horse-drawn] carts from the reserve, but old Rufus used to get the job of going out in the bush and cutting the rails and that and bringing them in on this old T-model Ford. Yes, I can remember that.

For the bough covering we just used ordinary old coolabah trees there because it was too far to go and get the budda bush and cane-grass. The leaves from the coolabahs was good shade. We used to put enough leaves on. It was only the later years when they got sort of modern motor cars and that, that things started looking up a bit on the reserve. They used to go out to North Bourke and cut the rails and the coolabah and cart it back in and make the bough sheds out of that, but they don't have them anymore. That's all finished.

All the water for the people on the reserve came from the river. Joanie and I … it was our job to get the water. We had an old grey horse named Nodical. Yes, Nodical. We used to hook him up to a forky branch, like a sled, and go down the river and bucket into this couple of hundred gallons tank, then pull it up to the house. Sometimes, we would leave it there on the sled, or bucket it into 24-gallon drums. Most times, we used to just leave it and just dip the water out of it for washing up and having a bogie in.[8] It was much easier when we moved up town; running water. There was no running water on the reserve in those days.

There was water in town. There was a big waterworks there behind where we used to live. It is all houses there now, but it used to be all vacant block behind Tudor Street, but, there was only a couple of houses there then. Now it is all houses right to the riverbank. The old waterworks is still there. They treat the water out of the river. It goes through a treatment there, a treatment plant.

That horse died. Old Nodical died before the move from the reserve to town. When not using him we'd just let him go. He used to just hang around the camp, yes. He would never go far away.

I can remember a few people that came to the reserve. One old bloke in particular, old Bob Hubbard. He was blind. I do not know where Bob came from, but my old grandfather, he used to take pity on these people. You know, they would travel around carrying their swag and that. They would come to the reserve and nowhere to stay and he used to take pity on them and take them in. Another bloke was Walter Thompson. Another bloke was 'arry Boney.

Walter Thompson, he had a brother, Les Thompson, but there was two Les Thompsons. One from Nockatunga. I think old Walter and his brother Les came from South Australia where old Duck Johnson came from. They come from that way, but they were fullbloods. They were real black.

They came from somewhere over Coopers Creek way, I suppose. Yes, one bloke, he was covered in sores, I can remember. They used to call it Barcoo rot and my old grandfather went out and got a quinine bush and boiled it and used to bath him in it. In about a week he was all cleared up. He stayed with us

8. An Aboriginal term meaning swim, bath or wash. The word is commonly used in the outback.

then. Well, he nursed my oldest sister, so he was with us for a long time, old, old Walter Thompson. He went to the war with old Alf Hagan, old Uncle Alf.

Alf was in the Light Horse Brigade or something, yes because they were horsemen. Old Uncle Alf he was reared up at … He lived in Nockatunga when he was only a boy. Yes, he comes from there. He was born at Quilpie though, I think, but he was reared up around *Nockatunga*. He was reared up by his uncle old Jimmy Smith, but old Uncle Alf, he had the marks, the tribal marks, cut on him.

Now, about my two sisters. Well, Junie's two years older than Joanie, and Joanie's three years older than me. So, Joanie would've been born in '37 and Junie would've been born in '35 and the Cullen girls and the Hagans [Alf and his wife Janet] they took the three Cullen girls, of old Mickey Cullen, but Mickey Cullen was a white bloke, but he married a dark woman from the reserve there. Well, she [Mrs Cullen] died. Their mother died same as our mother and old Mickey was in the army too, but he didn't go overseas; he was in Sydney. I don't know what he done, but he didn't go overseas and the Hagans finished up adopting them and they had the six of us. There was Maisie Cullen, Margaret Cullen and Olive Cullen.

They didn't really adopt them properly. They took care of them. I mean, see they never changed their name, they were still Cullen, the same as us [staying Gray]. I mean, we never had our names changed, you know, we went under … When Mum married George Gray, the English bloke, well we just took [kept] his name.

I wouldn't have a clue what stations my father worked on. I know on my birth certificate it says he was a station hand, but I can remember him saying when he first came out to Australia from England he worked in the mines in Broken Hill. Then he moved to Bourke somehow or other and met Mum, and he worked on the stations and then he was a grader driver. He wouldn't go home [to England]. He transferred to Wyong and he was 72 when he retired, 96 when he died. Had a pretty good innings, yes, but he sort of left us behind. When he went down … and Joanie went down to Wyong, I think, not long after. I didn't see her for a few years.

She came back when she was eighteen. She was down there for about three or four years and came back out to Brooksville and lived with us. We used to do a lot of fencing out at Brooksville. I can remember Joanie and I with the old stroller. When the car broke down we had no way of getting the iron posts [star pickets] onto the [fence] line. We pulled all the canvas off the old stroller and I used to put the rope around my neck and she used to push it. We'd put two iron posts in the wheels and pull them over the sandhills and old Uncle Alf used to carry the big gidgee strainers on his back. He was only a man about … he wouldn't have weighed any more than about 9 stone [57 kg] so the gidgee strainers were pretty big.

There was always a lot of funny things happening in Bourke, but nothing that comes to mind straight away. Yes, a lot of bad things. I mean some of the old blackfellas there … there was one old bloke, what was his name? Gilbert his name was, his surname was Gilbert, yes. He used to get into trouble a lot with the police through the grog. They came down once there and they said, 'We come down to take you up to the gaol.' He come down in the side-car, this copper did, and Gilbert wouldn't go, and he said, 'Well, you've got to come,' and Gilbert said, 'Well, who's going to make me?' so the policeman pulled a gun on him. He said, 'Me and this fellow here,' and pointed the gun at him, so he went. He was one of the bad old blokes. He didn't cause so much trouble in the camp, but when he went up town and hit on the grog he'd end up getting into fights with the white people up town and they'd go and report him, and then the police would come looking for him. He used to stay with us mostly.

Gypsies and Afghans

We used to have a lot of shows. The rodeo that I can remember … the gypsies used to come there with the travelling sideshows and they took my auntie when she was a young girl, and her uncle. It was Auntie Janet, Janet Knight, the one that married Alf Hagan. They took her and, anyway, they chased them down and they got them back. They went and reported it [to the police]. Her father, old George, and a couple of other people – I think it might've been one of his brothers, old Harry, and old Archie too – they went with the police and they were on the road heading towards, going back towards Sydney. They chased them down and Auntie Janet was in one of the caravans with Val Knight; he was a lot younger than Auntie Janet.

I can remember the old Afghans, even they used to try and get kids. In the old days there was a lot of Afghans in Bourke. I can remember a few of them. A while back I read in a book about a woman, Mrs Perooz. I can remember her. She lived in Bourke for years and she was married to an Afghan, or was it her father was Afghan? I knew Mrs Perooz.

I remember the camels being there, but I don't remember them coming in, like loaded up and things like that. No, I don't remember that, but I know they were still there in Bourke, because you used to see them. Old Arjune was one of the Afghans and he had camels. He lived there, in Bourke. His old camel wagon was on a big vacant block behind our house up in Tudor Street. That's where he left his old wagon. I don't know whatever happened to it. I never seen it there, you know, like later on, but I know it used to be there when we lived in Tudor Street. Somebody's probably taken it away or tried to restore it, or something; a big old camel wagon.

The wagons were very heavy, because they used to put bales of wool on them, see, to carry the wool. The camels and the bullocks they did the same sort of thing, but I mean, they're very, very heavy, the loaded wagons. I still can remember the camels there in the yard, but I never seen them hooked up to the wagon. I think they might've been some of his favourites he didn't want to part with or something.

Mrs Perooz she had a shop there later on. It was right down towards the end of town, towards the reserve. She had a shop there for a long time and then she sold it to Auntie Betty, Betty Knight, Ngaka Ebsworth's wife, and Jeannie Mackie, they went in partnerships and they bought that shop and then I think Auntie Betty sold out to Jeannie. Well, as far as I know Jeannie's still got the shop there today. Just smallgoods, but she, you know, mostly the blackfellas go there because it's close to the reserve. It is not in Oxley Street. I think it's only one street back towards the town from Adelaide Street.

The Public School

We went to the convent school for three years and then we moved up town and went to the public school and I can remember this teacher. He didn't like black kids very much, and – Keith Howie his name was – and they used to have the roll-call every morning and this bloke used to put me down as absent, but I was in school all the time. Then the Welfare went and saw my auntie, Auntie Janet, and said, 'Well, he's been wagging school,' and I swear on a stack of Bibles I never ever wagged school, you know, but he used to put me down as absent, trying to get me into trouble with the Welfare. Back in those days, you see, the Welfare used to send you to the home or whatever, and anyway, it never dawned on me what he was doing until I grew up. Gee, I never wagged school and this bloke was putting me down as absent, you know, in the roll book.

When we moved up town in the '40s, we were still going to the convent school and then it was too far. See, we was right up in Tudor Street and the convent school was right down on the old billabong, so the old auntie decided to change our school to the public. Joanie and I went there for a while. By then Junie was working at the Gables, the Gables boarding house. She was a housemaid there. Later on, old George, my father, he moved to Wyong. Joanie was about fifteen I think when he moved to Wyong. She went down there with him and I stayed with old uncle and auntie and we moved to Enngonia.

There were times there in Bourke we used to go out to Toorale. Old Uncle Alf used to work on Toorale station and then it started getting cut up into smaller blocks and then he took a job more or less boundary riding. It was at a place called Lake Mere and all of us kids used to go out there during the school holidays. I remember once there at this Lake Mere … it was all big red sandhills and Junie and Joanie and myself we used to go up onto this great big high thing and slip down. I was only a little tack and I went over behind the bush and I had me strides off and they sung out, 'Camel,' and I took off with me trousers in me hands sliding down this big sandhill and Junie and Joanie was sort of half the way down the sandhill. They were running and there was camels there. They used to come in. There are still camels on Toorale. I'll never forget that. I was running flat strap swinging me trousers and I wasn't going to pull up to put them on because the camels were there.

We used to hear stories about them when the bull came in season they got really savage. Because I'd heard that so many times I was a bit scared of them and so was Junie and Joanie. That's why they took off and left me. I was only about five or six, or something.

One bloke there at school called me a 'black b' [bastard] once and I had to, you know, I was always taught to stick up for myself, so I give him a punch-up. Then he went and told the teacher and the teacher asked me why I thumped him and I told the teacher why and I still got into trouble over it. I still got the cane, but I used to hate being called a black so-and-so, I mean it's, I mean, not only me but all the blackfellas are like that, they don't like being called 'black bs'.

It was a woman teacher. She said, 'What did you hit him for?' I forget the boy, I think his name was Rumble, Robbie Rumble, and this was at the public school and it was over a cricket ball or a cricket bat, or something. Anyway he called me a 'black b' and I just punched him and then the teacher asked me why and I told her, but she still gave me the cane though; three on each hand with the feather duster. Yes, but that was back in those days.

Enngonia and Station Work

I left the public school because of work. It was too far for the old uncle to come back and forward when we left Toorale. Ken Stulley had bought a place out 60 miles [approximately 100 km] east of Enngonia and he [Alf Hagan] wanted to shift the family out there. We sold our house …

[Ken Stulley's place was called] Brooksville station. Yes, about 60 miles east of Enngonia. Anyway, we went there. We went to Brooksville first and then the Welfare got onto them too about taking me away from school. I remember at Auntie Betty's place, they [school officials] came there because I was working with Uncle Alf. We started fencing and contract mustering and breaking in horses and that.

I was twelve when I left school but I went to Enngonia for about two to three months and then I went full-time with fencing and mustering with old Uncle Alf out at Brooksville.

The school didn't worry, as long as I was working. They didn't worry, but they would've if I was running around the reserve like, doing nothing, but I was helping him [Alf]. Like working for him and he used to give me … I mean he bought all me clothes and he always put money aside for me, but I was learning things. Then after a while there I was back and forwards, like on and off I took other jobs on. I was fourteen when I left to take a job at Ellerslie, but only on and off, you know. I'd go there for a while and then I'd go back to the old uncle then back again. I think I was about sixteen when I actually went full-time at

Ellerslie and he was back and forwards. He had all the work, contract mustering and fencing, yard building for Miley, just the other side of Enngonia, out as far as Brooksville, Widgee Downs, Talbalba, that was on the border fence. We used to do a lot of fencing there and after bushfires, like we'd get repair work. It was a heap of work back in those days. You was never short of a quid, never short of a job, not like today.

Junie left before we ever moved out there. Joanie and I were still going to school. Junie left when she was about … She was working at the Gables as a housemaid and then she met Roy Smith. Unknown to the old uncle and auntie she sort of told a couple of fibs to get away from home, and said she had this job at the store at Enngonia, but she was going out there for her boyfriend and they started living together. They eventually got married in a church and they had twelve kids, boys and girls.

Roy Smith, well he used to be Roy Shillingsworth. I mean there was a big mix-up there because his old father … Sometimes his father used to go under Smith and sometimes under Shillingsworth, so the kids were the same and even today … well, one bloke in particular, Lyle, sometimes if he got into trouble with the police he would say, 'Well, I'm Lyle Edwards' and another time he'd say, 'Well, I'm Lyle Smith' and other times he'd say, 'Well, I'm Lyle Shillingsworth.' They'd do that, yes, but I think now that most of them go under 'Smith'. I mean their mother and father's dead. They call the Aboriginal reserve, where the old reserve used to be, they call that after their mother Alice, you see her name was Alice Edwards and now they call it Alice Edwards Village.

At Bourke on the reserve, yes and another place they've got there named after Alf Edwards, her brother. He was about the oldest, I think, in the family, and when he died they got his park there now. In Bourke they call it Alf Edwards Park, that's down the reserve in Adelaide Street. Down the west of town.

Joanie went … like she lived with the old man down in Wyong for a long time and then she came back when she was about eighteen and she came with us. We was out at Brooksville, then Enngonia, and she came back and worked for us for a couple of years, I suppose, or twelve months. I forget now but we came into Bourke once and she got appendicitis and she had to go into hospital and we couldn't, you know, stand around there, so we went back to work and

Pat Simmons, Turk Shillingsworth/Smith and Billy Gray outside his sister Joan's camp at the Engonnia Aboriginal camp (usually referred to by the whites as 'the blacks camp'), 1959. Fire shows typical cooking method the people had to use. There was only one borewater tap for the entire camp. This was Joan Gray's fire outside her hut.

worked out at Brooksville fencing and then we came back in to pick her up. Then she had a job in a cafe; she was working in the cafe. In Old Peter's I they called it. Old Peter and Tully, Italian blokes they were. It was in the main street of Bourke, in Oxley Street.

They [the Italians] also had the White Rose, that was Pippos. Old Pippos used to own that and then they [Peter and Tully] had that other one we used to call 'Peter's', known as the blackfellas' café. The two old brothers they owned that and Joanie used to work there and she didn't want to come back, didn't want to come back out in the bush and that's when she left home.

Singalong outside Joan Gray's hut at Joan's Camp, Enngonia. L to R: Dawn Edwards (later, Smith) on guitar, Jim Smith, Pierce Edwards (squatting), Pat Simmons (standing), Joan Gray, Turk Shillingsworth/Smith (squatting in doorway), Colin Gee (squatting), Billy Gray, and Charlie Edwards (squatting on right).

We left her in town there and she was there working for a while. Actually she was living with a bloke that I used to work for, Billy Howlett, and his wife, and she was boarding with them and then she was engaged to get married to Harry Martin from Cunnamulla. We were invited in for the wedding – we was still out at Brooksville – and we were invited in for the wedding and we got into Bourke that night in the old Chev we used to have, an old Chev ute, and drove down to the camp and Harry was walking around crying. Joanie was nowhere to be found, she was gone. She took off. She went over to Brewarrina. That's when she met Sonny Orcher. It was very strange because we went in for the wedding and the bride was gone; she flew the coop!

I hadn't seen her then for about, gee, four years I suppose she was over there and I used to write to her at Weilmoringle. She went to Weilmoringle because Sonny was a shearer. Back then he was a lot younger. He was a very good shearer and crutcher and that, and he followed the shed work all the time, but mostly around Weilmoringle, Brewarrina, Goodooga. Well Joanie and I used to keep in touch. She'd write and I'd write to her and then we lost old Auntie Janet. Joanie came home for the funeral and she never went back then, she stayed with old uncle [at Ellerslie] Well, he was at Ellerslie and I'd left Ellerslie, like we'd both started work there, but he used to go backwards and forwards like I said

Billy, about sixteen years of age, at Ellerslie station, near Enngonia, 1955/56.

before. He had, like, Brooksville, Glenora and all those places. He used to do the contract mustering and that, but he more or less came back to Brooksville and was permanent there, but when they wanted him, he'd go like to other places around. But he always had a job. He left Ellerslie and he got a job managing a place just out of Bourke called Warella Plains. Warella Plains, behind the Native Dog Bore there. He went out there and he was managing that and I'd left Ellerslie then. In the meantime I went droving. I was about sixteen when I left Ellerslie. Yes, I was about sixteen because I went to Bourke and I mated up with an old bloke called Ray Gordon and we turned out to be good mates. He had a job with old Cecil Kenny at Fords Bridge and I got the job horse tailing. Ray was a lot older than me. Yes, he was. Ray was in his twenties, well in his twenties, yes.

There was three sisters that owned Ellerslie. One was married to Balcombe, old Bill Balcombe. They lived in Sydney. One was married to Frank Robertson. There was three sisters that owned Ellerslie. Hughie Balcombe, he came up there because his mother was one of the sisters that owned the place and, anyway, he came up there. He was there when I was there. He was the bloke that was managing the place and then he bought his own place and now, right now, Malcolm Robertson, Hughie's cousin, he owns the place now. They own another place out from Enngonia too.

I'd just left school, about twelve, and it was one of the times when we used to come in from Brooksville. Like when the old auntie would get pregnant out in the bush we'd have to come into town to wait until she had the baby, and it was one of these times. We was camped out at North Bourke and there was about three or four camps along there. Most of them, like the same thing, we'd come into town for the women to have their babies and I was letting off sneakers all day. And I was sitting on this drum, four-gallon tin that had no top on it and, of course, well I could feel it coming on and I thought well, 'I'll just let it go,' you know. Thought it'd be another sneaker but it ended up pretty loud and sort of rung in the drum and I got into trouble over that. I was pretty embarrassed.

I got into trouble over that from old Uncle Alf. Yes, I know it was only natural [to break wind], but I was pretty embarrassed too.

Droving and Photo of Mother

Old uncle, he was managing that place at Warella Plains. I went away and I was droving and that was in 1957. So I was about seventeen then, although I thought I was two years older, but I wasn't. At the time I thought I was nineteen and I was only seventeen. I went away with Billy Howlett and we was [on the road] for 21 weeks. We went out onto ... there was a place there we done three weeks contract mustering and we finished that and then he got the job to go out to the other side of Wanaaring to pick up a mob of sheep.

I forget the name of the place, but this place out the other side of Wanaaring, this is when I got the photo of me mum off Amy Johnson. That's the time we went to get that mob of sheep and we was on the road from the time we left Bourke. We done the three weeks contract mustering and then we went out to the other side of Wanaaring and mustered the sheep there and then started on the road. We went down what they call the 'cut line' from Wanaaring to Louth. From Louth to, what was the next place from there, heading towards Tottenham? Bobadah, and they sold the sheep there and the bloke, Georgie Shovel, he pulled out because we was camping on 24 hour reserves, like with the sheep trying to just kill time. Just feeding them along, that's what we were travelling for.

This bloke George Shovel he didn't know, but we were only getting 14 quid [pounds] a week and keep, you know, and that's in the '50s. He got on the grog and decided he wanted to go back to Bourke. He got a taxi from Tottenham to

Bourke and he had a note for Billy's wife to go to the stock and station agency to get his money and they wouldn't give it to him.

So he got in the taxi and he came all the way back and in the meantime the sheep had been sold and we were sort of packing up to go home. He'd brought Digger Gordon, old Ray's brother, he brought him down to help take the plant[9] back in an old rubber-tyred buggy. It so happens that I was the only one who saw the trip right out and it was 21 weeks from the time we left Bourke to the time I got home. Yes, so I was worried about my money because there was a lot of money coming to me and I was worried about that, but the bloke that I worked for, old Billy Howlett, he was pretty fair dinkum and he paid me right up. It was over 200 quid, it was a lot of money in those days.

We went from Tottenham, across to Nyngan and then up the highway. I can remember one little place we came to, I think it was Coolabah, we got caught in the rain and we just didn't want to get out of bed to put up the tarpaulin. So we drug our swags underneath the buggy and the water run through and wet the swags. Yes, I'll never forget that. It wasn't enough to trouble us. We just slept in our swags, we didn't give up, me and old Digger Gordon. Bill Howlett was married to Digger and Ray's sister. It turned out Joanie used to live with them before, long time ago, like I told you. Anyway, I went back to Bourke.

We had about 28, 30, or something horses. Yes, everything was carried in the rubber-tyred buggy, all the food, swags, all the old ropes that we made, like, for the break to put the sheep in.[10] They were all there and made, it was easy to carry them; you could roll them up and put them in a corn bag and throw them on the back of the buggy. But I went back to Ellerslie after that, too. I used to go back, you know, for a few months. Could always get a job back there when you wasn't doing anything.

---

9. A drover's plant consists of all the droving gear, including cooking utensils, tools, horses and associated items, swags, tucker, working dogs and vehicle (sometimes pack horses). Billy was referring to all the gear that fitted into the buggy. As usual the horses would have had to be walked back.
10. Ropes, sometimes wire, were used to hold the sheep in breaks at night. In those days there were often breaks formed from fallen mulga called a brush yard. A break was usually three fence-like legs forming three sides of a square or rectangle. The fourth side kept the sheep in by using a roll of wire or staking dogs along this line. Often the camp was also made along this leg. Mulga breaks were a common sight in the droving days.

Learning to Ride

Old Uncle Alf, he was a very smart man, like stock-wise, and used to throw me on buckjumpers.

I was about five when we were out at Toorale, at Lake Mere. I used to cry then though, and my sister, Joanie, she used to laugh, because she was a fairly plump girl, you know. I can always remember it. Like, he would throw me on this horse and the horse would start pig jumping [also known as pigrooting], throw me off, and then he would pick me up and throw me back on, and I can remember Joanie standing there. She was like a jelly on a plate; she was just shaking with laughter. Yes, and I was crying because I'd get thrown from this buckjumper.

The old uncle would say, 'You've got to learn to ride, mate. This is the way you're going to make your living. You've got to learn to do a bit of a pig jump, that's not bad. I got learnt the same way.' His old uncle, Jimmy Smith, he used to throw him on buckjumpers when he was a kid too.

My uncle never drank in his life, no. He was one of the few that didn't around Bourke. Most of them used to have a bit now and again, but no, he was one bloke that never did. I can remember one old bloke – what was his name – Mungindi, Mungindi Jack or Jack Mungindi? He was a fullblood and he was one of these fellows that was a born-again Christian, and he used to be a bit of a plonko. Anyway, he was sitting around – all the boys down the camp, they had a few flagons there and he was sitting around – they were all sitting around drinking you see, and 'cause old Mungindi was there and I think he might have been tonguing for a drink, but anyway, the boys said, 'You going to have a drink with us Jack?' and he said, 'Well, you know, I'm a Christian'. He said, 'Yes, but I will have a drink.' Then one of the blokes sort of pointed up in the sky and said, 'Hey, Jack, what about that fella up there?' like meaning God. He said, 'He'll see you.' 'No,' he said, 'I'll get in there underneath that fly there and that is where he won't see me'. I thought that was a classic.

Argument and Family Deaths

I went back to Enngonia, back and forwards. My old uncle, when we were at Ellerslie, we had a bit of an argument over a dog once. And this Bawley – his name was Bawley – and I'm trying to yard these sheep and this Bawley kept getting in the front of the sheep and they were breaking. It was stinking hot and I had hold of a .22 [rifle] in my hand and I swore at his dog. And he [Alf] jumped the fence and broke a gidgee stick and he was going to flog me with this gidgee stick. Anyway, I took off, but I wasn't quite quick enough. Anyway, I spun around with the gun and I said, 'You come another step and I'll blow you over.' Of course, doing that, that just made things worse and he had a 25.20 [Winchester rifle], and he just walked up to me and, of course, he'd learnt unarmed combat in the army when he was in the war, and he just chopped me to pieces with the butt of his gun.

I had the .22 and he had the 25.20 and he took mine off me. I was a big lump of a kid then. I was about, I suppose, sixteen, sixteen or seventeen, something like that, no, I would have been sixteen. He put me down to the ground. Anyway I got away from him. I took off and he chased me in the Land Rover and I tried to dodge him in the scrub, you know, in the Land Rover and old auntie was swinging on the side there trying to stop us. The funny thing, he never tried to give me a hiding after that. It was the first time I ever stood up to him.

He was very strict. I mean, you had to be brought up that way. Like, he knew best I suppose. I don't know, but I thank him for it because he was the only father I really knew, but he was only an uncle by marriage and, I mean, he went without a lot of things for me. You know, like clothes-wise. We would go into town and he would make sure I had everything first, before he would buy anything for himself.

He was a very good man. Very strict, but I used to cop it with a rubber hose and gidgee sticks, but I still don't hate him for it. I never drank until I was well in my twenties.

Auntie Janet died when I was on the road [droving]. She had taken sick on Ellerslie and was being taken into Bourke on a truck when she died. I was at Waltara, public watering place on the Wanaaring Road.[11] That was when we were coming in with a mob of sheep. This is the same trip that I mentioned earlier, and old Ray came out, Ray and his sister, Billy's wife, and told me what had happened, so I went back in. But the old Brother Southwell, he was a preacher and mostly for the dark people … and they came out in his truck and picked me up to take me back into Bourke for the funeral. And old Ray, he took my place [droving]. He started cooking. I was horse tailing at first, but when I went back to Bourke for the funeral, old Ray took the cooking over from Georgie Shovel and Georgie started doing the horse tailing. I was gone a week and then I came back and caught them up, in old Charlie Cox's taxi. I got a taxi back to work and Ray and I paid half each. I came back to work and he had taken my place for a week and he went back with the taxi, you see. The fare wasn't a great lot, as they weren't far away. You could only do about five, six mile a day with the sheep; travelling for feed. Yes, back in the good old days.

Yes, that was her funeral. And by the time we finished the trip – and, as I said, like, it was 21 weeks – old Uncle Alf he lost his father in Cunnamulla, only a few months after he'd lost his wife. I didn't get back for that. Then two months after that he died, old Uncle Alf. I think it must have been the strain on him, I mean, losing his wife and then losing his father, you know, only a couple of months apart.

He died of a heart attack. He was only in his forties. I'm not sure, but I know he wasn't 50. Yes, 47, 48, something like that. She was only about, well, she was in her thirties when she died, but she had a bad heart because it was in the family. All the Knights have got bad hearts. Some of them died young.

---

11. Public watering places were also referred to as government bores. They were located on travelling stock reserves, along stock routes.

Yes, those three people, within four months, yes. Yes, and then when he died I came back because I'd been on the road.

When he died I had to come in for the funeral and old Ray took my place. Yes, it was bad for the old fellow because he … I don't think his … old ticker … because he worked hard, although he never drank, but he smoked a lot and it was just too much for him. His kids, Dorothy and Barry and Dawn and Daphne, they sort of went with Junie. Junie had them at first and then the priest, old Southwell, he took them though Junie wanted to keep them. Yes, the Hagan children were taken by Welfare. Brother Southwell and them were like missionaries, probably Bush Brothers. They used to go down to the reserve and that and have Sunday school and take the people up in a big truck. Take them up to the church, have cups of teas and, you know, like trying to …

I went to Enngonia in, I think, it was '58, '57 … '58 Christmas. I went out to Enngonia after I finished around Bourke there, droving and that. I went out to Enngonia because Junie and Joanie lived there and I was mustering the common there for a bloke called Georgie Smith. They used to own the grocery store in Enngonia and he had all his sheep and cattle running on the common and he had to take them out. So I got the job mustering the common for him and, then this was about a week before Christmas, and his old uncle, an old bloke, Alec Cuffe, he used to own New Park [north of Barringun, running along the border on the Queensland side]. He rang up and he asked Georgie to send him up a bloke to do some delving on the bore drains and that. So I got that job and I went up there for a week and ended up staying there three-and-a-half years. It was quite good actually.

Droving and Strange Things in the Night

Going back, I can remember once, I was only about fourteen, and we delivered a mob of sheep to a place … I just forget the name of the place, but I think it was Quantambone. It was over round Brewarrina, and there was three of us on the road. There was myself and old Uncle Alf and Walter Thompson, 'cause they were pretty good old mates from the war, and he used to work with us mostly. Yes, and we had to take the horses back and the old uncle left me with the packhorse with a heap of tucker and that and I had to tail the horses back on my own and he gave me a mud map with all the camps I was supposed to have along the route on the way home. He drew me a mud map with a bit of charcoal on paper. He said, 'Well, the first night out you'll camp here and the second night you'll camp there,' and so on and so on. And one of the camps was an old hut. During the night I thought – well, I thought it was – it sounded like a baby crying at first. Yes, I heard this noise and I got out of bed and my old uncle used to say, 'Well, before you run, have a look to see what it was. Make sure it was not a ghost.' So I'm scared, but anyway, I climbed up and it was coming from the ceiling in this hut and I climbed up and it was a bloody koala. It was a baby koala and they sound just like a baby when they cry, you know. And that's what it was. All the hair on the back of my head was standing up, but I was determined to see what the noise was before I run, 'cause like the old story about what happened at the shooting gallery [clay-pigeon range] there in Bourke, at the old rifle range there. A bloke went in there once and he was sitting down, laying in his swag, and this is what I mean about noises. Like, if you heard a noise you'd always make sure what it was. This bloke, he said, 'Who's that in there?' or 'What's that?' or something, and a voice said, 'There's only me and you here, mate.' And he said, 'Well, when I get my boots on it'll be only you here.'[12] He was ready to take off, that bloke. Another time back at Ellerslie there, at Dunsandle – Dunsandle and Ellerslie were very close together, they're just separated by the boundary fence – where old Harry Conroy was breeding quarter horses and so he gave us these four horses to break in. One of them was a little tiny bay filly for his daughter, and it had to be really quiet. Well, me being the smallest and the lightest, I had to do the riding. And I can remember once when we were walking these horses – we had them for about eight or nine weeks, to really quieten them down – and this little horse, Cinderella he used to call her, and I was chasing these sheep. You used to have to have a crupper on her because she was so small. Anyway she ducked her head and started pigrooting and lifted her tail up and the crupper came over and the girth broke and I went spearing straight into a rabbit burrow. I can still remember that. I came up with a mouth full of red dirt and I was spitting red dirt and dust out of my mouth. The old uncle was just sitting back on his horse laughing at me. I'll never forget it. We even done a trip with those four horses, actually. We done a droving trip with them from Brooksville to Brewarrina, because old Conroy wanted them quiet. So the old uncle had a good name for all his breaking-in out that way, because he used to really quieten the horses down and work them right down, you know, to send them back. But everybody appreciated his work out there because he used to do a good job.

I remember old Walter Thompson was with us, that trip, and one night we camped on that Nineteen Mile Plain just out of Brewarrina. They used to say there was min min lights there, and we all sat up this night looking for the min min lights, yes.[13] Well, it was No Tree Plain they called it. I mean, it was nineteen mile across and not a tree on it. We put in these iron pegs. Everybody had a guess to where the sun was going to come up and there was three of us. We had three iron pegs each and we had lined them up to where we reckoned the sun was going to come up. It so happened, anyway, the old uncle was the closest, but <u>we were not far</u> out, you know, only about, well, I mean, not too far out.

12. Apparently taken from Edward Harrington's poem 'Only the Two of Us Here'.
13. The min min is a mysterious light that is seen in outback Queensland. Many reports of the phenomenon have come from around the township of Boulia, the Channel and Diamantina Country.

No, we didn't see any min mins that night. We sat up all night, nearly, waiting for these min min lights and we never saw anything.

No, and I've never seen them. I have seen lights but I do not know what they were. I got a bit of a fright once. This was when I was working for the Yanks. We was out around St George up in Queensland doing exploration, oil exploration. I was going home, because all the young fellows used to go into town [after work], and I had a Mark II Zephyr car, and I was going back after being nearly all night in town. It was about 3 o'clock in the morning and I saw this light in this dry creek. I do not know what it was but, I tell you what, it put the wind up me, mate, and I put the foot down.

No, it wasn't a fire, it was moving. It was keeping pace with me. It was going along with the creek on my right hand side of the car. I always said it was a flying saucer or one of them UFOs. Gee, that was back around about the mid-'60s, about '66, '67, yes. Well, it looked like a fire, but, I mean, it was moving. You know, it was just a glow there in the creek and it kept pace with me for about a mile and then just disappeared.[14] I always thought it was a UFO. I wasn't hanging around to find out, anyway.

---

14. Many people have described this as how min min lights behave.

Injury, Swearing and Tucker from the River

Getting back to Bourke and that. One time we went to meet the train – Bourke was the end of the line from Sydney – and old Uncle Alf was coming back on leave and we had to go and meet the train in the old horse and cart we had. I was cutting wood this day for the old auntie. I had my tongue out, and I missed the block and the axe handle came up and hit me under the chin and my teeth went through the middle of my tongue. I've still got the scar there to prove it. Yeah, I remember sitting on the buggy seat up at the railway line, at the railway station, and the old uncle came back, yes. Oh, it was painful, too. Oh, it bled, yeah.[15]

Sometimes we used to get firewood in like that, but old Curley Rumble, he had a taxi cab in Bourke and he also had the wood yard. He used to go and cart it in and cut it up on the saw, like into blocks, and we used to buy it off him. All good gidgee wood.

You know, a lot of the time, like, things that happened back in those day … I mean, a lot of the things like the way the kids were brought up. Like if the old people were sitting around yarning or talking, if any of the kids came close they would, you know, there was no warning, you just wasn't supposed to be there. They'd jump up and go for you. There was no warning. You wasn't allowed to go near the old people like that. They reckoned you were ear dropping [*sic*] on them and it wasn't right.

---

15. If this occurred in 1945 or even 1946 Billy was only five or six years of age. In those days it was common for children of that age to be cutting wood with an axe to help while the man of the house was absent.

And when I swore, that was deadly. I mean, you'd get a hiding, the old razor strap. Many a times I got it.

Yeah, very strict people in those days. I mean, you go back there today and see how the young people are living. I mean, back when I was a boy there, if you got caught hanging around a pub, anybody, any of the old people that knew you, you'd get a hiding for it. They'd go home and tell your parents or your people what you'd been seen doing. They sort of … all the old people used to do that. That old Charlie Phillip, he was a bad old egg for that. If he heard anybody giving cheek to their parents or any grown-ups he used to chase you with a rope. He'd pull you up and bash you. Put the rope around you, yeah, he did that to Auntie Nita, Uncle 'Ope's wife, pulled her up in the shed, yeah … up around your neck. Yeah, pull you up off the ground and, I mean, you'd be choking and your tongue would be sticking out. But he knew how far to go. You know, as soon as he saw you going a bit blue, then he'd let you go. I remember another time there when we were all playing down in the billabong there. When the flood had come up there was one big hole down the reserve that used to fill up with water. It used to stay like that and there was a lot of booglies [yabbies] there and we used to go down with some cotton with a bit of meat on it and an old net and scoop them out; then throw them in the fire and eat them. Our parents used to sing out, 'Come on, get out of the water,' late in the afternoon and once we saw old Charlie coming with that rope we used to make a beeline for home then.

Those booglies were real big ones. Blue shell; real blue and about six to eight inches [approx. 150–200 mm] long. They were beautiful. Yeah, good tucker. The real old, good old tucker.

Back in those days, I mean, people used to live on fish back in the late '40s, early '50s. I can remember the weir there. Uncle 'Ope and I and old Uncle Alf Hagan used to go down there early in the morning, just on daylight, and you'd look over the side of the weir and it'd be just a black mass of fish. We had a net and we had an old single bed, just the frame, and we had a bit of netting tied around it and it was my job to get in the middle, and they'd get on either end and we'd walk around in the water and we'd have a job to lift the thing out on to the bank. It was full of fish. We ate fish every way possible you could cook it: you know, in the mud, in the ground, like in curries, fry it, grill it, every way possible.

Yeah, and it was good for you, too. Didn't know that in those days, but it was good for you. I used to love yellowbelly and bream.[16] Yeah, mostly yellowbelly, but we used to get the bream and the catfish, but mostly yellowbelly. One fish that I'd never mistake was the old yellowbelly; yellowbelly and catfish.

We also caught [Murray] cod. Not there, like that, not with the net, but with the hand lines. Yes, we used to catch the cod. For bait we used shrimp and worm; the big old blue worms you used to dig out of the garden. Well, you'd go out, you'd shoot a bird or something with your shanghai. You'd shoot a galah or magpie or something and pluck it and throw it in an old kerosene tin and put a few holes in it and tie the bird or whatever you had, sometimes a bit of meat, and tie it in the bottom of the bucket and you used to throw it in and leave it for ten minutes, fifteen minutes, and you'd always get shrimps to put on your line.

Fish back in those days were plenty. I mean, you go up there now, most of the time you get a lot of carp, but not as much as before. They are starting to die out a bit, you know, the carp, but you still go back looking for the old yellowbelly.

Kangaroo, emu, porcupine were good tucker. Yeah, you'd only have to go five mile out of town to get a feed of wild meat, mostly kangaroo. We used to use dogs. We'd go out with old Percy Rolfe and Granny Nellie, she was a Knight. We used to call her Granny Nellie and she was crippled, always in a wheelchair. She'd had rheumatic fever or polio, I think, when she was a kid, or something. I don't know what it was, but she was always in a wheelchair. We used to go out to the, I forget the name of that bore, it was the last one coming in on the Fords Bridge Road, the last one coming towards Bourke. Well, he used to look after that; he was the caretaker there, old Percy Rolfe, and they used to have a little jinker, what they called a spring cart, but we used to call it a jinker, and it was only just a two-seater vehicle. Yes, one horse drawn. I remember going over all the broken ground, you know, the cracky ground there [dry, blacksoil country]. On that road there it is all broken, big cracks and holes and that and the kangaroo dogs would be trotting along in the shade of the buggy or the sulky or the jinker, or whatever you like to call it, and me and Joanie would sit on the back. In the broken ground old Percy would say, 'You better jump off for a while, kids,' and we'd run along with the dogs because it was too rough.

---

16. Bream is a common name for the silver perch (*Bidyanus bidyanus*).

But they were marvellous little vehicles. I mean, they was light. You know, the horses could pull them anywhere.

They had rubber tyres. Pneumatic tyres like a small car. They were 100 percent on the steel rimmed wheels. They were still in use then, too, the spring cart with the iron wheels on them. Yeah, old Lennie Johnson, old Norto we used to call him, he had one of them and he was the transport when they used to take us out to the 'halfway'.[17] If a flood came in Bourke there, the police and army used to come and shift us out on the sand, to the halfway, and he was our transport. It was a fairly big buggy, iron wheel one. Yeah, he had, I think, three horses, I think; three-horse-drawn.

I remember this one horse, because old Norto used to have … like, it sounded like he had something in his throat all the time when he talked, and he used to have this one horse. I think it might have been his favourite. He used to call it Rose and I could always remember him when we'd all jump in this old buggy and go into town and he'd, 'Come on, Rose,' and old Rose would just lay into the traces and pull it, pull the buggy along.

---

17. The halfway was the red sandhill country between Bourke and North Bourke.

Personalities and Old Customs

Yeah, it was unreal, for us kids, you know, we used to … I can remember once at the halfway there, this old king … I don't know what he was, King Wally, or something. I know he had a big brass plate hanging around his neck. The first time I saw him, this was in the 1950 flood, he was sitting at the corner of the police station with his little dilly bag and his little swag. Anyway, King Wally, or something, I don't what his name was, I forget, anyway, he came out there to the flooded river. He used to go down and he'd light a little fire and he'd corroboree and he'd be talking the lingo and singing the lingo and he'd point these fire sticks at the flood and he reckons he was hunting the water away, like, making the flood go down. So, all of us kids, we used to go and put a stick in at the edge of the water, like, where the water was. We'd poke a stick in the ground and we'd go back next day expecting to see the water was like falling back away from the stick, but it would be about two or three foot past the stick, so he wasn't doing much good with the old tribal way of hunting the water.

Another thing like they used to do in those days, too, the old people, like the old fullbloods. They used to … if a big storm was coming you could see it out there on the plains, you could see a big storm rolling in and they'd get old Granny Nelly who was another one that done this, too. She used to sit in her wheelchair and her arms were sort of like, her hands were like sort of crooked from the polio or whatever she had, the fever she had, and she used to spit towards the cloud to hunt it away. They reckoned that when you done that, the old people would spit at the storm, you know, to make it go past or to go around. They believed it.

Storms and floods were called *ugun* in the lingo. So they'd say, 'Look out, there's a big ugan coming', like the floodwater coming down or the storm … big rain. Sort of meant the one thing.

Like, in Bourke there we used to call the white person *whydgebulla* and 60 mile up the Darling at Brewarrina they used to call them *gubbas*. You see, that's the difference, and, I mean, only 60 miles apart. There was so many different …

And funerals, oh mate, that was something that you could … I mean, it was very, very creepy, you know, like, one would start up … One person would start in the camp in the lingo and then they'd all take it up and it was like just one big hum. Like, one would start and then another one and it would go right through the camp and all you could hear was just one big hum, you know, in the lingo. I don't know what it was, what it meant, but I can remember it and it used to make the hairs stand up on the back of your neck. It was really creepy. It'd go for all night, the next day even, in daylight. They'd be crying and they'd be singing. One bloke in particular, old Jack O'Lantern,[18] he was one bloke that I can remember. If you mentioned anybody, like, just recently passed on, he'd start singing. Him and his wife would start singing straight away. It was very frightening. Just like a moan or a howling, just continuous. It sounded like they never took a breath, it'd just go on and on and on.

Jack O'Lantern and another fella, Jimmy Siddick, they used to frighten young girls. Uncle 'Ope, he used to tell me a lot because he was older than me. They used to frighten the young girls by threatening to point the bone, you know – mostly out on the stations – like they wanted to get her away so they could …. Yes, have sex with her. They'd frighten them. They'd say, 'Well, if you don't come, I'll point the bone, I'll sing you,' and the girls used to get that frightened that they used to go, they'd sneak out and let the old blokes have their way with them.

---

18. In his book *The Dark People of Bourke* (1978), Max Kamien says that Jack O'Lantern, a fullblood from Weilmoringle, 'was widely regarded by other Aborigines as having healing powers.' He said that he knew of three people who could not obtain relief from Western drugs, but 'all were cured after Mr O'Lantern removed the "sickness-causing foreign bodies" from their heads.' Billy, who thought O'Lantern came from Nockatunga, pronounced O'Lantern as 'Lantrum'. See also note on p. 74 for Bert Powell.

A lot of the white blokes used to use the girls that were out on the stations and that. They used to do the same, not the same thing, but they'd find ways of getting the girls outside or getting them away from the house; talk the girls into sneaking to their quarters and things like that. A lot of them used to do that.

I can remember back on the Bourke reserve there, there was some white people living there, an old bloke and his son, and their names were Taylor, and I learnt from my old mate Chris Woodland, he told me that they were related to Ben Hall or that family.[19] They used to live there on the reserve. His son was Percy, and I think the old bloke's name was Bill or Jack Taylor, I'm not sure. When his old father died Percy left Bourke and I've never ever seen him since. That would have been back in the late '40s or mid-'40s; just after the war, anyway.

Percy was only a big lump of a boy about seventeen, eighteen, nineteen or something like that. But they used to mix with the Murris [Aboriginals] down there. Then, the other old bloke, like, old Fred Hull, he was a bloke that bought the shop off old George Knight. He was sort of bent over; he had a humpy back. Something happened to his back, I don't know, he got thrown off a horse or something, but he used to walk sort of bent over. He had family in Bourke but they wouldn't recognise him, for some reason. His brother was a plumber, because I can remember him coming to Brooksville when he put in a … when the spray dips first come out, you know? We used to have the old plunge dips and then the latest stuff came out, the spray dip. Old Ted Hull was the bloke that came out, him and his son Les. They came out to Brooksville and put the spray dip in. We was working there then; we was building the sheep yard there, actually.

The Taylors lived just like us at the reserve. In an old tin shack, yes, made out of the old kerosene tins; dirt floor. They used to have a horse and cart the same as us. They had a lot of dogs I can remember. I think he might have been a drover. I'm sort of scratching my mind. I can remember him there and I can remember him having a lot of horses. I can remember him having goats, because we used to … well, I was reared on goat's milk and I think Joanie was reared on goat's milk, and we had a lot of goats when we was down the reserve. I know that we

---

19. Jim Taylor and bushranger Ben Hall's wife Bridget (nee Walsh) left the Forbes district and settled at Fords Bridge about 70 kilometres north-west of Bourke. It is not known for certain if it is the same Taylor family as the one that had earlier been connected to the bushranger.

got some off him, I think, to start. Actually, the old grandfather got them and he started, but we used to milk them, because we was reared on goat's milk.

I think just about everybody around Bourke in those days had a go at droving. You know, they'd try it out and some would sort of wait for a job and others wouldn't wait, like the Johnsons, old Norto [Lenny Johnson] and Stevie Johnson. I think Stevie Johnson's still alive; I'm nearly sure he is. But all the others … I know Amy's still there.

Well, old Gus Potter was one of them [a boss drover]. He had a really big plant and a lot of horses. Who was the other bloke? Old Saffey, old Bill Saffey. He used to have a fairly big plant. A lot of the blokes come from interstate. When the Bourke meatworks was going, like, a lot of big plants used to come from way up north. You know, they used to come down and bring cattle down to the meatworks. Some of them were big drovers but they'd never hang around, they'd go straight home. Benny Wilson was another bloke that done a bit. Old Gus Potter was a white drover

I don't think the Hodges done much droving. I know they had stock there. They had a few stock running in the common, because they used to use … they used to call them 'leaders' [also known as Judas bullocks]. They used to take … they had one big bullock with a bell on and he used to lead the cattle over the North Bourke bridge and take them right up around behind the halfway there, right up around to the meatworks. The bullock used to walk in the yard and he'd make a complete circle of the yard and he'd come back and he'd stand at the gate, and when the last bullock went in he used to go out the gate and go home; go back to North Bourke about four or five mile away. Old Mrs Hodge, they used to live down in between town and the reserve once, but they moved out to North Bourke. One of the sons was named Gidgee. Gidgee is still alive. He lives in Dubbo now. The other fellow, the older bloke, he still lives down way out at North Bourke there, but not where his mother and father used to be. He built another tin shack. He still lives like they used to, like dirt floor, no power. Actually, I went past his place when I went back to Bourke in '86. I went back there and I went out to North Bourke looking for a good fishing spot and I drove past his camp. I didn't even know he was there. Anyway, he came down and we started talking, because he knew a lot of my people. Yes, he was a white bloke. But I forget his name, that bloke, but he used to work at the meatworks.

I'll never forget his smell, because I don't think he bathed very much. He used to work in the tallow room at the meatworks and ride his pushbike all the way into town. Like, from the boning room they used to take all the bone and, like, when they'd bone all the carcasses … Actually I was working there as a barrow boy. I used to push all the bones out into the tallow room and put them into these big pressure cookers and they'd cook it up to make the blood and bone and the fertiliser and all that stuff. Well, this old Hodge bloke, he used to work there, and you can imagine the smell. I mean, it'd nearly make you sick. And he'd wear the same clothes for four or five days, so you can imagine … no wonder the man never got married, because I don't think he'd find a woman that'd put up with the smell.

Me and my first wife, we worked there [Tancred Meat Works] on and off for about 12 months. That was when I left New Park. That was around the end of '60, '61.

Euley Brown, he was on the reserve, too. He came from Nockatunga. He married one of the Eulos, but he was promised to … I'd don't know what you'd call it, but up in his part of the country you were sort of promised to a girl, or a girl was promised to you and you wasn't allowed to marry anybody outside that arrangement. But somewhere along the line, he met one of these Eulos and, anyway, he ended up living with her and he came down to Enngonia. I can remember because he used to tape a knife to his hand. He'd tape a knife and he'd sleep with it. Like, he'd lay on the knife, sleep on his belly and lay on the knife. They call them kadaitcha or thenagoolia or feather men, those blokes who were supposed to be after him; whatever you like to call them. He was scared they'd come hunting for him because they would have took him back or killed him; one or the other. Yes, they wasn't allowed to marry outside of their tribe, but he was one that did. There was another bloke, too, Les Thompson. Not the Les Thompson, the one that we knew, but this was another bloke. I don't know where he came from. I think he came from up there too, somewhere. Well, that'll be the bloke, the crooked neck Les Thompson. He had something wrong with his neck. Apparently he used to get flogged with a hobble chain and that's what hurt his neck or something.[20]

---

20. Chris Woodland was told in 1960 that the Aboriginals from Nockatunga were 'good blacks'. Many years later Chris asked Jim Kiley, one-time drover and poet of Bourke, what would have been meant by such a statement. Jim replied that the blacks had been treated severely at Nockatunga and if mistakes were made they were treated harshly. Without Les Thompson's name being mentioned, Jim referred to 'crooked neck' Les Thompson having been belted across the neck with horse hobbles as a child.

The old uncle, see, he was reared up around … Old Uncle Alf, he was reared up around Nockatunga and he reckons that he was reared up with … Jimmy Smith reared him up and he never had much to do with the white bosses. But he had the tribal marks on him, old Uncle Alf. He had the marks on his chest where they 'barked' him. He had two on the chest, I think, one either side, and then he had one on his right arm, right up on the top of his shoulder. When they used to cut them, they'd cut them open and then they'd put the hot ash in and they used that, like, sort of for a medicine and to make the skin swell when it healed so the marks would never go away.[21]

Old Jimmy, see, his uncle, was a sort of, you know, old yellow fellow. He was sort of half-caste. Old uncle, old Albert, Albert Hagan was his father. The Hagans had Irish in them.

Hagan, an Irish name, yes. So there must have been, well they weren't real fullbloods. But he was pretty dark, old Uncle Alf. He was pretty dark. You see, back in those days they used to take them out when they become of age. They used to take them out at Nockatunga, he told me. All the old fellows would take you out into the scrub for a week or two and make a young man out of you. Like initiate you and have corroborees and that. No one was allowed to go to them. No women were allowed to go, only the old blokes. Then they'd bring you back into the camp and they'd give you to an old gin there in the camp and she'd be sort of real happy for the young boys. You know, she'd have the first night with them and sort of break them in. That was their custom.

My relations there, old Archie Knight and old Albert Knight, they were about the same age, you know, a few years apart. They used to work out around Willara and those places and I just forget the name of the property, but it was either Willara or Tinapagee or Nocoleche.[22] It was one of those places. They were both working at the same station, and this young girl was working there as a maid. Unknown to either of them, they were both sort of sharing her, but they didn't know they were. Anyway, they were sneaking – and this came from old Uncle Archie himself, he told me this – he said that he walked around the corner and he was looking up at the light trying to get into this girl's room.

---

21. The hot ash would sterilise the wound and prevent infection.
22. Both Tinapagee and Willara are in the Cuttaburra area, west of Bourke towards Wanaaring; Nocoleche is on the Paroo River, south of the Wanaaring road.

He'd wait till the light'd go out, see, so they could sneak in. It was a fairly high window, so they probably had to walk around through the door or something. Anyway, he was standing up against the wall waiting for the light to go out and then his brother came around the corner and stood right next to him. He said, 'What are you doing here?' And they were both doing the same thing, they were both sneaking to the same woman. Anyway, they both missed out that night because they sort of had a bit of a argument over it. The girl was sharing both of them. She didn't know which one she wanted. But I thought it was quite funny. That came from the horse's mouth, from old Uncle Archie himself. He told me that yarn.

The Knights go back a long way in Bourke, all around Wanaaring, Louth mostly. I don't think they ever went up Cunnamulla way. They were mostly around Bourke and Louth and Wanaaring. Because my mum was born in Wanaaring; my mother. I think her mother lived around Louth. I'm not sure. Well, I heard, like I said before, that her father was the policeman there in Louth, a German bloke. But, you see, as far back as I can remember the Knights, Uncle 'Ope, Opey Knight, he done … When the Aboriginal started to get a little bit of a say on what was going on in the community, he was one of the ones that got the houses built on the reserve. You see, they've got beautiful houses there now. All the old tin shacks are gone. But he was one of them, like him and a bloke called Noely Gillon were the two that sort of pushed the issue and got the houses.

Yes, that part there about Uncle 'Ope, he done a lot of work for the Aboriginals in Bourke with the houses and that, and a lot of court cases and that, he fought for them. He worked for the Legal Aid part of it and then he worked for the Widjeri,[23] like getting things for all the blackfellas around Bourke. Then when he died his daughter took over and she worked for the Widjeri and she done a lot when he died.

Yvonne Knight, Yvonne Howard, she married Bob Howard. He's a whitefella, but she done a lot there. She sort of … I think she was in a car smash or something and she had to give it away. Yes, she couldn't sit for long hours. But she done a lot for them and her son, now, he still works for the medical side of it. He works for Aboriginal Health, the one in Oxley Street there. Well Kevin,

---

23. Widjeri was an Aboriginal hall, since burnt down.

he does that, the third oldest in the family. He still works there, but I think Yvonne still does a little bit but she's not full time. She still helps out where she can. I think most of it's just voluntary work; she does it for nothing, just to help her people. But to look at them, I mean, you'd think they were white people, but they never ever said they were white. They'd always say they're black people, you know. They are really fair skinned.

Yes, old Percy [Smith], down the reserve. He was a great old bloke. He used to suffer from epileptic fits, but I can remember he used to make these little board men. He used to make them and they'd be all somehow attached to a board and string. He used to sit it on the edge of the old aluminium bathtub and tap it and this thing used to go up and down like it was tap dancing. All the kids there, we thought it was great. He'd sit down and he had this little tune he used to sort of do with his tongue and tap this piece of board out of an old tomato case or something, that real light wood, like real flat board, real thin. He used to play this little song with his tongue and tap-dance these little men. It was great for all of us kids. He used to just do it for us.

We used to make old steamrollers out of the treacle tins, you know, for our toys. We used to punch holes in either end and put a wire through them and hook them all up together. Sometimes we'd have sort of fifteen, twenty, steamrollers we used to call them, and make tracks all around the camp there, around the reserve.

We'd eat a lot of treacle, the old black treacle, yes, and the Golden Syrup. See, it come in the same … one tin was a reddish colour and the other one was a sort of green and gold. I can remember that. Johnnycake and treacle, or bread and fat, kangaroo and emu, fish, porcupine. Yes, I was only a little tacker then, but I can remember it. I can remember it like it was yesterday.

Old Bismarck, he came from Nockatunga and he was one of the blokes that believed in the bone [pointing]. He was very, very … well, Uncle Alf's mother, they reckon that he 'caught' her. Like, the old saying, like, if you were sick you got 'caught' by someone. By that they meant pointing the bone. Old Uncle Alf's mother, she was one of those believers. She was sitting under the bough shed and a piece of twig hit her on the head, like, fell on her head and she started getting headaches because she reckoned that he caught her and he pointed the bone at her. Anyway, it worried her to death. She died through it. Yes. Old Bismarck, he was one of them fellas. A very frightening looking old bloke, too, he was. I can remember him. I saw him once in Cunnamulla when we went up to Cunnamulla. The only time we used to go to Cunnamulla was for a funeral, from Bourke, when any of old Uncle Alf's people used to die. But old Jimmy, he got killed in a car smash going to Quilpie, a head-on smash with a truck. It killed him stone dead. I can remember going up for that funeral.

You see, all those old fellows they had something. They still practised the old ways when they could. They really spooked us young ones. They had some [power], like old Chrissy Siddick and them, and old Bismarck.

Chrissy Siddick was another fellow that used to threaten the girls, like, for sex and to get them away from the homesteads and that. But he looked … he had shocking eyes. I can remember him. Just to look at him would be enough to frighten you, old Siddick. Yes, some strange name, but he wasn't real black, you know, he was sort of a yellow fella.

Old Baker, old Baker Lucas, he was a sort of, you know, a real private person. He didn't like people coming around his place [at the reserve in Cunnamulla] or anything. A bloke come up to his gate once there and I don't know what he wanted, we just heard the story. Baker said, 'Well, if you come in my yard, I'll shoot you.' The bloke did, he went in his yard and Baker shot him all right. Baker got five years out of that.

Another old lady that got sent away, too – she got life – was Dougie Young's mother, old Vera Young. She hit a bloke with the leg off an iron bed and split him down the forehead and killed him. She got sent to Boggo Road in Queensland, in Brisbane, for life. She died in gaol. Just through grog. They were just having a blue of some sort and she whacked him in the forehead.

I can remember Dougie Young.[24] He used to come down with mobs of cattle from Cunnamulla. He used to work with Uncle Alf's brother, Freddy Hagan, and Bobby Hagan the older brother. They used to always come down from Cunnamulla with mobs of cattle for the meatworks at Bourke. The first time I met Dougie Young, we'd just moved up town. It wasn't long after we moved up town. As a matter of fact, it was Dougie Young and Freddy Hagan that bought

---

24. Dougie Young was a well-known Aboriginal songwriter and singer.

me my first pair of R.M. Williams riding boots, I can remember. Dougie used to have real smelly feet and he used to get me to put Johnson's baby powder on them for him. He left Cunnamulla, Dougie. I first met him when I was about eight. I was still going to school. I was proud of them, the first pair of R.M. Williams riding boots I had, and I've worn them [the brand] ever since.

Yes, he used to sing all the time, old Doug. A good guitar player, but his brother, too, Robert, the younger bloke, I mated up with him a long time after that. I hadn't seen Dougie Young for years, but then I end up marrying their cousin, Joanie McCarthy, in Cunnamulla. Her brother was Richard McCarthy. They used to call him Darby.[25] He was a champion jockey back in the '50s, no, in the '60s. He went to France. He rode in France; he was over there. He came back because of the climate. He had a bad chest and he couldn't fulfil the contract. So he only stayed there, I think, for about twelve months and he came home. But, yeah, he rode all over the world. He rode in France; he rode in the States; he rode in Singapore. Yes, a very good jockey. He won the Sydney Cup; he won the Brisbane Cup, the Doomben 10,000; the Metropolitan. He won all those big races. Now he lives in Toowoomba and I think he's teaching the young Aboriginal kids. He's got a stable there and he got a grant from the Aboriginal, I don't know what it is up there, but he's teaching the young kids to ride, anyway.

---

25. Darby McCarthy was a famous Aboriginal jockey. His story can be read in the book *Darby McCarthy: Against All Odds*, by Max Presnell, Melbourne Books, 2004.

Colourful Days at Enngonia Reserve

Turk Shillingsworth and Archie Knight were involved in a big fight around Enngonia in the late '50s. I wasn't there, but I heard. Archie told me himself that it was over the shearers. The shearers were racialists towards the camp blacks there, the Aboriginals, down at the camp.

It was something to do with the cricket match. It lasted, like, sort of all day and well into the next day. It sort of went all night. There was shots fired and all in that. Yeah, it was like a riot, you know. I know someone got shot and someone got a white bloke with a stick.[26]

You see, back at Enngonia in those days there the shearers, all the shearers used to come. I can remember when I was sort of in my teens and Lyle and myself and Archie and big Roger Hooper, we used to camp out on the back of an old Fargo truck. We used to roll our swags out in the back of the truck and the shearers would go to the pub, get a gutful of grog and then on their way back, like, over the river – because all the camps used to be along the road there down near the bridge – they used to sneak into the camp looking for women and come in drunk. I remember there we used to sool the dogs onto them of a night or early hours of the morning. Yeah, they walked straight into

---

26. Turk's brother was shot with ratshot from a .22 rifle on the Sunday when the whites were looking for Turk, who was lying on a very soft and sunken mattress in a hut, unseen by the searchers. A white man was hit with a cricket stump by one of the Aboriginals, possibly Archie Knight. On their return to the station at which they were employed that night Turk and Archie hid in the machinery shed when they heard a vehicle coming through the night. They were thankful it was Chris Woodland and Colin Gee returning from their evening kangaroo shoot and not possible pursuers from Enngonia.

the houses there, you know, like, the camp, looking for women. I mean, some of the women would wake up – one in particular, Betty Kelly, we used to call her Googie – she woke up and a bloke had her by the leg and she screamed out and they sort of took off and we heard them, it woke us up. And old Alice Edwards and them, and Reggie, they used to have big kangaroo dogs and I can remember Lyle and myself and big Roger Hooper, we sooled the dogs onto them and you could hear their … you couldn't see the truck but you could hear the doors slamming on the thing. They'd start up and take off; I can remember that. You know, they'd get a gutful of grog and thought they could do anything. You see, they treated them like dirt and they were dirt themselves. If you went and put the police on them nothing would happen, but if a blackfella went up town and started swearing or doing something up town, the police would come and lock him up. But the whitefellas got away with it.

At Enngonia there I remember once these four guys that came up from Sydney. It was Chris Woodland, Teddy Kilgour and Alan and Roy Gardner. These guys came from Sydney and they came out to … I was working at New Park. Anyway we went into town, went into Enngonia and they had the old hall, the dance hall, they made it into a picture theatre and I was pretty good friends with these blokes and, anyway, I wasn't allowed to go up and sit at the back, like, where the white people were. I had to go and sit right down the front. The bloke that had the thing [business] then he had the pub and he had the picture show and he was a shearing contractor. Yeah, I thought it was pretty weak. So did my mates, because I couldn't go back and sit with them. They used to throw – a lot of the white people used to throw the crumbs from their sandwiches or hot pies, whatever they were eating, they'd throw it over the piece of hessian bag they had up to separate the blacks from the whites, and they used to throw their crumbs and that over the hessian bag into where the blacks sat.[27]

I wasn't there when the Enngonia pub was burnt down in the early '60s, but there was two blokes involved with that. At that time, the pub had changed

---

27. The film showing that night was *Attila the Hun*, starring Anthony Quinn and Sophia Loren (1954). From the back the black people, who entered the front seats by a side door were unseen behind the hessian sheet that was spread from one side of the small building to the other. At times the film ran very slowly, making the actors' dialogue very slow, with a deep drawling effect. Though unseen there was much enjoyment and laughter from those down the front. In the spacious white-occupied section were some drunken ringers who sang out obscenities and rolled their empty beer bottles along the floor. It was said that the person running the picture show used to hire the films from Sydney for private viewing, but charged the entertainment-hungry locals two-and-sixpence admission.

hands and an ex-copper bought it. The black fellows used to go up – because they wasn't allowed in the bar – but they used to go up to the back door and get their plonk and that and their beer, and this ex-copper used to sell it to them. They'd go up there all hours of the night. He'd get sick of them and he wouldn't get out of bed to serve them and things like that, so they used to get cranky with him. There was two blokes that were blamed for it. It was Trevor Dutton and old Angus Woodgell. Old Angus was a fullblood but uneducated and people thought he was a bit silly, but I don't think he was silly, it was just the way he was brought up. Anyway, he ended up taking the blame for the whole lot and he got – I forget how many years he got – but he went to gaol. Trevor got out of it scot-free.

They went up and tried to get grog and he wouldn't serve them and so they just heaped the bushes up, like the budda bush there around Enngonia, I mean, there's plenty of it. They just scraped it up, because the old pub was an old wooden place, and they just threw a match into it and up she went. They only had the old fire engine, like, a tank on the back of the truck. The water came from the public bore, which was about a mile away from town. The truck had a little motor to drive it, a little pump. They had no chance. I mean, 60 mile would have been the closest big fire truck, which would be Bourke. So she just went up in smoke.

Angus went to gaol. I think Trevor sort of talked him into it when they were locked in the cell together and I think Trevor told him what to say. Well, this bloke, he had no idea and he told them what Trevor told him to say. He didn't know that he was going to go for a stretch. But anyway, it so happened he did. He got, I think it was about five years, I think, he got for that. Anyway, Trevor's, what? – he would be in his forties, I suppose – but to see the man now, he's crippled from the grog. He gets along; he's all right, he can get around when he's not drinking. He can't walk; just crippled up from the grog.

Another thing we used to do for amusement at Enngonia was the old claypan dance. Sometimes there we used to play rounders on the same claypan, big rounders. They used to love it. I used to like it myself and I was sort of, you know, nearly twenty then. My sister and all the other kids around the camp there they used to come down and play. But them old claypan dances of a night, especially on a Friday or Saturday night, and when you could get all the people

Playing rounders at the Enngonia Aboriginal camp. Col Gee's ute is beside Joan's camp. Billy is in checked shirt facing camera. Col is on far right and Turk Shillingsworth/Smith is squatting in green and white top. Note the black ground in the foreground made by the burning of tyres when the people held claypan dances.

together, like all the musicians. We had old Alf Edwards, he was good on the gum leaf and the old button accordion, and Dawnie, his step-daughter,[28] she used to play the guitar. Or one of old Alf's brothers, like, Cliff or Maurice, they used to play the guitar. Old Granny Evie used to play there, Eva Knight, she used to play the accordion

Yeah, the old button accordion. Old Alf, he could play both. He used to have the … they used to call it piano accordion. Sometimes, like I said, when you could get them all together. It sounded really good, like the mouth organ and the gum leaf and the button accordion, and the guitar, and we used to have a real shindig down there, because all the people that didn't drink, just for the … go there to enjoy yourself. And then the other boys sometimes, like, from the other end there, from the Eulo [mob] end, they used to come up and they'd be full of plonk and that and they'd start fighting. Of course, everybody would go home. The next day, then, the claypan was used for the settling ground. They used to come there then and sort their differences out.[29]

I remember Ike Andy and Uncle 'Ope. We was at the hall one night there – because black fellows wasn't allowed in the hall – but we used to go and stand around a fire. We knew most of the people, like, the white people, because we used to work around there. And they used to come out with, like, all the food that was left. Some of them, you know, was really good, and they'd come out

---

28. Dawn Edwards became Dawn Smith, having married Turk Shillingsworth/Smith.
29. Billy's sister Joanie told Chris Woodland that often drunken white blokes would come over to the claypan dance looking for women and making nuisances of themselves. An evening of laughter and general enjoyment for young and old would be ruined and terminated with the now despondent participants returning to their camps.

and give us all the sandwiches and that. So, me and Uncle 'Ope was billy boys there one night at the hall dance, because, like, we knew the blokes and they come out and said, 'Can you keep your eye on the coffee and the tea?' They used to boil it in a four-gallon tin.

So they gave us the tea and the coffee and we used to throw the coffee in the bucket and throw a couple of coals in there so all the coffee would settle to the bottom and the tea leaf; do the same with the tea leaf. Anyway, they used to bring all the food, like, that was left; sandwiches and cake and that. Ike Andy came there and he was drunk. Uncle 'Ope, he was a bare-knuckle champion of the western districts back in those days and he used to do a lot of bare-knuckle fighting. Ike wasn't bad himself, but he king hit Uncle 'Ope and Uncle 'Ope had a mouthful of sandwich when Ike hit him in the back of the neck and he sort of spat all the stuff out, like, the sandwich went whoosh out of his mouth and he turned around. It was dark, see, and he said, 'Who done that?' And Ike Andy's bouncing around like a bantam rooster.

Anyway, nothing come of it there so they stopped it and next morning they finished up on the claypan where we used to have the dances. Ike didn't last long; I think two hits and he was knocked out. But they used to go there and settle their differences. Not only them, I've seen plenty of fights there. I mean, when you'd see them going down … Everything was professionally done. They had the seconders, the referee, everything, but all bare-knuckle, though. When they'd sing out, 'Fight', or somebody would say, 'Fight', well all the camp would go. They'd all stand around just to watch the fight. I tell you what, mate, *TV Ringside* had nothing on it; it was as good as *TV Ringside*. And good fights, you know. They respected one another. Whoever got knocked over or knocked out, they'd get up and shake hands and say, 'Right, we'll have a drink later. That's it, it's all finished.' Yes, in the good old days they used to do that, but now they go for bottles and guns and sticks and stones and everything. But back in those days, it was not allowed. It was just bare-knuckle and that was the way to finish it. Of course, everybody got enjoyment out of it as well. Some of them used to finish up with black eyes and broken noses and split lips.

Back in those days you didn't wait long for a job, because there was so much work around. The blokes used to be willing to go out then, in those days, most of them. I'd say 95 percent of them would be willing to go to work. You'd ring up, like, if you came in from one job you'd think, 'Well, you know, these fellows out here'd be starting to do their mustering for lamb marking or shearing or crutching or something,' and you'd ring them up, and nine times out of ten you'd get a job, because there was plenty of it around.

There were big families at Enngonia. The biggest families was old Reggie and Alice … Well, he used to go under Smith and Shillingsworth, old Reggie; he married Alice Edwards. They had a big ring of kids. Actually, one of them, Roy, married my oldest sister. There was Shillingsworths, the Eulos – that was another big family – they were all fullbloods. They used to live up on the Bourke side of the reserve at Enngonia and sort of up over the rise. They more or less kept to themselves. Only when they got drunk … They come from up Nockatunga somewhere. You see, old Eulo, there was three sisters or two sisters and I can remember – what was their tribal names? One of them was – I said the names last night or yesterday – funny name. Anyway, old Bumpedy, she was old George Hart's wife, she was a Eulo. This Euley Brown, he was another bloke that married a Eulo. Old Jack Lantram, I think his wife was a Eulo. You see, they all come from way up that way, and they went from Nockatunga to Cunnamulla; Cunnamulla to Enngonia. They sort of drifted backwards and forwards there. Chrissy Siddick was another fellow that used to live there. But the big families was mostly the Shillingsworths, and the Shillingsworths are still there, a lot of them.

Edwards was another family, but the Edwards was scattered. They sort of … Bourke, Enngonia. But the big families, like the two biggest families there was Shillingsworth or Smiths, as they're now known, and the Eulos, but there was a few other little families, like a lot of them married into the Shillingsworths. A lot of them married into the Eulos and the Sullivans and the Browns and a lot of the Orchers come there from Weilmoringle and we had a big camp there back in the late '40s to the late '50s, you know, that was a big camp there. It would've been I'd say, at least, I don't know, 300 or 400 blackfellas in that camp, but they shifted that camp now out behind the cemetery. They've built houses there. Nice houses. Yes, they've got their own houses there, all water, like running water and everything.

We'd all wait for that Warrego [River] to come down and when that came down there was tucker galore. I mean fish and crayfish and booglies or yabbies, or whatever you want to call them. I mean everybody would go down with a net or, you know, and come back with a kerosene tin full, four gallons and put them on the fire and cook them up and have a big feed. Yes, it was good.

The huts were just dirt floor and tin. All old corrugated iron or whatever tin they could find, yes. A lot of the cockies [graziers or farmers] around there used to give them any old tin laying around the stations close to Enngonia. They used to give it to them or the people that'd work out there they'd buy if off them and bring it in to build a house, 'cause I bought all the stuff there for my sister [Joan] from O'Malleys, just up the road from Enngonia there. I saw the tin there when I went out there for something and I saw all the corrugated iron and I said, 'Well, how much do you want [for it]?' Anyway, I got it pretty cheap and got somebody to go and pick it up for me and my sister got blocks to put her house up there for her.

For water they only had one tap on the reserve at Enngonia. One tap and, well, because he was the first one there I suppose it was old Reggie Shillingsworth. He built his house right alongside the tap. He was cunning. It was bore water and then all the rest had to, like there was houses all around. We used to carry ours when we lived there. We used to cart ours in the 44-gallon drums, but we had a truck. I remember we used to come in from Brooksville after mustering, shearing, or something, 'cause like I said before, we done all the contract mustering and we used to find, you know, all these emu eggs and old Uncle Alf and Walter Thomson and myself we used to take our old pair of trousers on the back of the horse and get the emu eggs and put them in the leg and separate them with a piece of string so they wouldn't get broken. We'd do this all through the season, like when the emu season was on. We'd, like, drop the eggs down in the trouser's leg. Tie the bottom of the trouser leg with the string and have them hanging over the neck of the horse; like straddle it.

We had an old fridge box.[30] It was an old fridge box we had on the back of the truck and when we were coming into town we'd fill this box with sawdust from the saw bench at Brooksville and we had all the emu eggs in that. And we'd

---

30. This would have been the remains of an old kerosene operated refrigerator. This particular incident exemplifies the utilisation of the limited resources available.

come into town and old Uncle Alf used to – you'd always think of the old people there in the camp and I was about fourteen, thirteen, fourteen something like that, and he used to say to me, 'Righto boy,' he said, 'Jump in that truck,' he said, 'and go around and give all the old people a feed of the eggs.' I'd go around to all the camps and I'd pick up somebody like Lyle Shillingsworth or Archie Knight, or somebody, and they'd stand on the back and we'd go around and we'd pass all these … We also used to always shoot kangaroos when coming into town, you know, and put them on the back of the truck and gut them and that, and leave the skin on them and bring it in like fresh, then drive around the camp and give all the people a feed. All the old people that couldn't get out and fend for themselves, but the old uncle was like that. He used to always think about the old people.

Yes, I used to have the job there. I used to make pocket money on the side carting wood there for the camp. Yes, I used to say, 'Well, I'd give you a drive of the truck if you'd come with me,' and I'd pick up all the boys. Turk and Jim and Lyle [all Shillingsworths] and Archie Knight and myself, all big young kids. Alf Hagan used to lend me the truck. Like, he'd let me do it for myself, like for pocket-money, and I used to charge them like two or three quid, you know, for half a load or something, because over the years, like you had to go further away from town to get your wood, see, because they used to just go out and cart it in the early days with a horse and cart. Then when people started getting cars they used to cart the wood. Well you were getting further away see and I used to go out with the truck – because we had a fairly big truck – and three or four axes and go out there and cut all the wood and load it on and come back and then, you know, like somebody'd say, 'Give me three quid's worth or two quid's worth'. Like we'd go around in the truck and I used to do well out of it for pocket money. I'd make, you know, sort of twenty quid on a weekend. It was good, yes.

That was when we were fencing, yard building, yes, all around there, at Brooksville and Ellerslie and Glenora, Widgee Downs, Talbalba; a lot of places all out that way, all around the 60, 70 miles from Enngonia.

Visit to Sydney, Araluen and Nerrigundah

I got to New Park in me late teens and I met a bloke, that's where I met me old mate Chris Woodland in '59, and I remember we used to go pig shooting and that. Another bloke, Teddy Kilgour, came up the first time I met Chris, and they invited me down to Sydney for Christmas; the first time I went to the big smoke. I caught the old steam train from Bourke and Teddy met me at the Central railway in Sydney and I didn't know him, he had a big leather apron on. He was a truck driver, used to carry spuds from the wharf and I jumped out of the train with me guitar and me suitcase and Teddy met me there on the platform, I didn't know him and he come up and grabbed me and said, 'Owi,' and I nearly dropped dead because I was a bit wary of these city slickers; I wasn't used to the big smoke, mate. First time in me life. Yes, and I stayed with Teddy that time and then the next year I went down and I stayed with Chris.

We went everywhere. They took me around to the … they took me to the Harbour Bridge. They took me down to a place called Araluen.[31] We went down there for, I think it was three or four days, shooting.

They also took me to Nerrigundah. My girlfriend, we were writing to one another and that was old Ray Gordon's sister. Her name was Stella, and Teddy took me to Nerrigundah and I picked her up and we were going to get married.

---

31. The picturesque Araluen Valley was a very productive goldfield area. It is situated about 25 kilometres south of Braidwood, NSW.

Pat Simmons and Billy singing by a campfire, New Park, 1959.

I took her back to Bourke, but she met somebody else because I went back to work, back to Brooksville, then to New Park.

How I come to meet Stella was they moved from Brewarrina to Bourke and Stella was only about fifteen, fifteen or sixteen, and she was working in the same old cafe that Joanie worked in. Anyway, all the young blokes used to try and get dates with the young girls, so I asked her for a date. Anyway, she let me take her home and then they moved. They moved to Nerrigundah because her people, old Mrs Gordon's people, lived in Nerrigundah. I don't know how they got down there but anyway they went.

They reckon that Jimmy Little the singer used to live at Nerrigundah, well he might be some relation to the Gordons, because old Mrs Gordon she come from down that way and old Gordon himself he come from Brewarrina. I don't know how he met her, but anyway, they had a few kids.

Billy beside the Araluen Creek, near Braidwood, NSW, c. 1960. It shows him in a landscape more verdant than his usual environment.

Splinter Reynolds and Bert 'Murri' Powell

The people used to come into town [Bourke], like, when the women were having babies. Yes, used to come in from the outstations, and that. There's one old bloke in particular, Splinter Reynolds his name was, and he was married to one of the Eulos from Enngonia. Anyway, he came in and he was booking his wife into the Bourke Hospital, and of course he had to fill in a form and the sister in the hospital was taking all his particulars and said, 'Mr Reynolds, what's your occupation?' Well, he didn't know what occupation meant, so he said, 'I'm a Catholic.' Well, she sort of scratched her head, the old sister, down at the hospital, and she said, 'Well, what's your religion?' and he said, 'Oh, I do a bit of crutching, a bit of shearing …' He was a fullblood, he was a fullblood. Yes, old Splinter Reynolds, yes. I'll never forget it him.

Bertie Powell, he was a fullblood. He was working on New Park when I went there; old Bertie. He was there before me. Like I said before, I went there for a week and ended up staying three-and-a-half years. Old Bertie, Old Murri we used to call him, he was a good old bloke. He learnt me to make boomerangs actually and he was really good at it. All the tools he had was an old bent-over shear blade, broken bottles, a bit of sandpaper, old tommy-axe, or tommyhawk he used to call it, and him and I used to go out and he'd say, 'Now, this is how you cut the root out, boy,' and I was pretty interested in it.

Anyway, we'd cut this mulga root out and he'd come back and … I've got photos of him, actually, but Old Bertie's dead now. He used to make the boomerangs for the exhibits. He'd put them in the show in Cunnamulla. In the few years that I knew Old Bertie, I think he put them in twice and both years he won the best exhibits in the show with his boomerangs and spears, and woomeras and whip handles and nulla nullas Yes, all that ringed gidgee [he used]. Whip handles were good out of ringed gidgee. Walking sticks, he used to make; but he was a good craftsman. He was really good. Old man, but he would sit down there for hours on a weekend when he was not working like Saturday afternoon and Sunday. He would sit on down near the old tree out the back of up there. He would sit down there. He would chip away and chip away and you would see this piece of wood taking shape, and he would feel it and he would balance it and he would put it up to his head. He would wave it around. 'Yes, she is coming along good, coming along good.' He would sit there for hours making all these things, yes.

Yes, Old Bertie used to like to make all these boomerangs. He was an old man. He would be well into his sixties then. The rumour had it that he was born about 1895. He used to always talk about Rocky [Rockhampton] and about the Carnarvon Gorge, or right up the top there. He drove cattle all over the place. Yes, into the territory there. Up into … Lake Nash, all those places, yes. A good, old horseman and a good old stockman, although he was starting to slow down a bit because he was getting on. I will never forget the day – actually the day that the boys left and my mates, Chris Woodland and the other fellas that were there, and I said, 'Gee,' they are good blokes, ain't they, Bert?' Bert said to me, 'Yes, they wasn't bad for whitefellas.' I will never forget that. Yes, he said, 'They wasn't bad for whitefellas.'

Bertie and I were … we were cutting wood and old Alec Cuffe, the boss, he dropped us off from the Land Rover with our axes and dinner bag and that. Old Mrs Cuffe used to make us sandwiches to take for our lunch. We were cutting wood in between, well, it was eighteen miles to the shearing shed from the homestead, and old Alec dropped us off in a good clump of gidgee. We were cutting the wood into cords and just stacking it and then pick it up later on in the truck,[32] but Bert and I were swinging the axe away there, the old Kelly.[33]

I saw this smoke. I thought, 'I wonder what that old fellow is doing over there?' Anyway, I kept working away, working away there, and about an hour

---

32. A cord is a bundle of wood made of logs or split logs measuring 4 feet wide by 4 feet high by 8 feet long.
33. Kelly was a brand name for an axe, which became a generic term for the implement.

Billy and Bert Powell killing a beast for meat, New Park, 1959.

Bert Powell setting out with saddle- and pack-horse to check New Park's boundaries. In 1965 he visited Sydney with other fullblood friends as Rainmakers in an attempt to break a severe drought. Sometimes referred to as Bertie, he preferred being called 'Murri', his own people's name for themselves.

Bert 'Murri' Powell making a boomerang near the single men's hut, New Park station, Barringun, 1959. Bert was a fullblood, born about 1895. It is thought he was born at Nockatunga in far southwest Queensland. Bert was very adept at making things, including boomerangs and whip handles.

and a half or two hours passed. Old Bertie sung out, 'Hey boy, are you hungry?' I said, 'Yes, I'm getting a bit that way.' He said, 'Well, how about we have a feed? Have our dinner now?' and he said, 'Come over here.' So I walked over and he had this porkypine [echidna] cooked in the hole.[34] He had got a porkypine out of the whole log and he dug the hole there and that was the fire I saw. I tell you what, mate, it was cooked to perfection.

It was beautiful. He had no knife, but he had his sharp axe and he quilled it with the axe. I mean, you scrape them with the knife to get the quills off, but the way he done it in the hole, the old blackfella's way, he fixed her up and he had a few stones there. He had hunted around there and found a few stones and put them in the ground. By gee, it was nice. We told old, Mrs Cuffe about it and she said, 'Gee, I'd love to taste porcupine.' She said, 'I've always heard about Aboriginals and how nice they were.' Yes, another time, he got a plain turkey [bustard.]. We had our own tucker and he said he wanted a feed of wild tucker. So we got the turkey and took it home and Mrs Cuffe cooked it for us.

They had a taste of that, but Bertie and I had the most of it. Yes, that was all right too. Yes, I think sometimes, I think, you know, you never knew what he was going to come up with. Sometimes I would think, 'Well, next thing he would have a snake in the hole.' Because he was real – the real fullblood. I will never forget the time me and Chris and him walked over to the camp. There was somebody going back from Enngonia to Cunnamulla and they were camped over at the public bore straight out from the station on the main road.

Old Bertie started talking in the lingo. He said to Chris, he said, 'Hey, boy, I've got you now.' He said, 'You can't understand what I'm talking about.' Chris had a good laugh. Yes, and I had a good laugh. I could not understand him either. Do you remember that?

He got one over you there, did he not?

Yes, poor old Bertie. Then things sort of got a bit slack. Old Mr Cuffe, he was saying that one of us had to go, but, he said, he hinted at it a few times, that things were a bit slackened off. Old Bertie used to say to me, 'He'll keep you on, boy, because you can drive all these tractors and all the machinery and you can

---

34. Porcupine is usually pronounced 'porkypine' by Aboriginal people.

fix them up and all this sort of thing.' I said, 'No, Bertie, you were the first one here. I think you should stay.' He said, 'No, I'll poke back to Cunnamulla there and I'll be there and when the busy times come I'll come back again,' and he did. He came back for shearing.

He stayed about three or four weeks and then he had a bit of a break again. He came two or three times there when I was there.

[Bert, or Bertie, Powell, preferred to be called 'Murri', a Queensland Aboriginal term for themselves. His interesting life, which began about 1895 went from the tribal days though to station work, droving to places as far as Lake Nash in the Northern Territory to Rockhampton where he lived for some years between droving trips. At Rocky, as he affectionately referred to the town, he was sometimes called on by the police as a tracker and actually found a murder weapon for the police following the murder of a woman by her husband. He spent a long time searching for the weapon and was finally rewarded by following a trail of ants where he found the bloodstained knife lying where it had been thrown in a vertical position amongst the growth of a sugar cane plant. During the Depression he had lived with some white men collecting possum skins in the Carnarvon Ranges. During a severe drought in Sydney he, Robin Quartpot Campbell, Jack O'Lantern and Shillin' Jackson went from Weilmoringle in September 1965 and did a rain dance at the Sydney Water Board in the hope of breaking the drought. Old Murri was buried at Weilmoringle later in the '60s. – CW]

Marriage

I left [New Park] in, what, '63. I left there and I went into the meatworks there for a while in Bourke. I worked there for a while, me and my wife. I got married in the meantime.

I was at New Park when I met her; met her at Cunnamulla. She used to work on a station. I was saving up to buy a car.

I forget which station. It was about 30, 40 miles out of Cunnamulla on the Bollon road. I was saving up to buy a car and I ended up buying a … I was all for a Holden ute. I wanted … All the young cockie's sons and that, they all had Holden utes, so I thought I would be as good as them. I had my mind set on a Holden ute. Mrs Cuffe's niece, she came up from Sydney. She was a schoolteacher in Sydney. She had a little Volkswagen and she had only just bought it. It was new.

Anyway, Mrs Cuffe had told her that I was saving for a car. She suggested I try the Volkswagen out. So she gave me the keys and she said, 'Take it for a run,' you know, to see what it was like, and I did. I took it for a run down to Barringun and back. I fell in love with it. So when I went into town, when I had saved enough money, I bought a new Volkswagen. I was the only blackfella around Bourke and Enngonia that was driving a new car at the time. I was really pleased with that, yes. I forget her name, that girl, but she was sort of in her early twenties, mid-twenties, and I know she was a teacher.

Yes, back in Bourke in the '50s there, I can remember some of the blackfellas used to have to have a … they could not go in the pub and that. Most of the boys used to get white people, like some of the blokes they worked with or shearers that came in from sheds and stayed at pubs, they used to go and get them to buy their grog for them, because, they were not allowed in the pub. They used to have to have a card they called a citizen's rights.[35] I can remember there was two people in Bourke that had them – and I saw these tickets – it was old Archie Knight and old Bertie Bates.

Old Bertie Bates was a fullblood. He married a white woman. Sheila Haythorn her name was. They used to live at the pound yard there in Bourke. They were the only two people that ever had those tickets. When I was at New Park, I often thought of getting one of these things for myself, because, the postmaster at Enngonia used to be an ambulance driver in Bourke, a bloke by the name of Noel McClelland, and I was going to get him … because you had to have a couple of people to sort of give you a reference. I thought of getting one myself, but it was starting to die out then. I was going to get Noel McClelland and Chris Woodland to sign or give me this reference – character reference – to get one of these things, but it started to die out so I did not really go on with it. You used to still get knocked back though in the pubs. I never drank, but, I used to go with Uncle 'Ope a lot, because they would take him for a whitefella. They thought he was white, but he did not have any trouble getting into pubs and that. He used to always say, 'Well, come with me and we'll go for a beer.' I would drink lemonade, but he would have a few beers and that. Yes, I remember once there, we came in with a mob of cattle and Sammy Davis … we used to call him Sammy Davis Junior, but he was about 6 foot 6 [inches]. He was like a big beanpole, he was. He was the tallest white man I had ever seen in my life.

He was like a whip, you know, straight up and down, he was that skinny. Anyway, we used to call him Sammy Davis Junior. I mean Sammy Davis Junior was black and short and this bloke was six foot six and, like, you know, straight up and down. Yes, we used to call him Sammy Davis just for a nickname. His right name was Sambo Franklin. Uncle 'Ope was working for him. They came in with a mob of cattle and camped out at May's Bend, just out of North Bourke.

It was just when – we used to call them 'Balts'[36] – they used to come to Bourke

---

35. Billy was most likely referring to the Certificate of Exemption which related to individual Aboriginals being exempted from the Aborigines Protection Act and all its restrictions.
36. Balts refer to the new settlers who migrated to Australia after World War II from the countries around the Baltic Sea, such as Lithuania, Latvia and Estonia.

back in the '50s. They used to try and get all the dark women, you know, try and get them drunk and then take them home and use them and let them go. These blokes were in this pub, the old Federal. The Federal now has been burnt down, but it is a motel now, just a motel. There is no hotel there anymore. They were drinking there and … It is on the North Bourke, Brewarrina road going straight out of town. It used to be on the corner where I bought my new car. It was straight across from the Volkswagen garage, but that now is a fast food place. It is all closed down, see. Anyway, these fellows were in the bar there this night and they were talking in their language, these Balts, and I can remember a big blue started there and Sambo and Uncle 'Ope was in this blue. We had horses there because we rode in from North Bourke. I was not working for him, but, I was just hanging around with Uncle 'Ope. Anyway, they chased them from there to the park [Central Park] with the stockwhips. They had stockwhips on their saddles. They jumped on the horses and these blokes were running down the street and Uncle 'Ope and Sambo were behind them with the whips and chopping them around the legs.

They were blueing with Uncle 'Ope and Sambo. I do not know what over, but, I mean, they were. Uncle 'Ope and Sam, they were young blokes like in their early twenties, like 23, 24, 25, something like that. It did not take much for them to have a blue, because that was just a way of life in those days, because they used to love having a blue. But, they flogged these blokes right to the park gate and they could not get their horses in through the gate. So they got away from them, yes. I can remember, like this is how strange things are.

When those fellows came to Bourke, those Balts, when they come to Bourke they were from overseas, new people, and the government turned around and built them houses, you know, for shelter, for them, but the old blackfella was still living in the tin hut down the reserve. Never done nothing for the blackfella, but, those people that came out here … I mean, they were not even from this country.

You cannot blame them, but, I mean, that is just how weak it is. You can imagine how the blackfella felt, because he was living there all his life and been a native of Australia and not having anything done for him back in those days. Yes, we were living down the reserve in tin huts and these fellows got big … like a big dormitory made ... well, they housed them. There must have been about, I do not know, 40 or 50 of them there. They started work at the meatworks and they started work on the railway. They were good workers. A lot of them started fencing. Not so much station work. I mean, they were not good stockmen, but good labourers, like at the meatworks and the railway and fencing, yard building ... roads. Some of them were on the DMR. There was one bloke there, what was his name? He worked at the meatworks when I was there. Now he owns half of Bourke. He bought the Gables. The Gables boarding house near where the Federal Hotel is just down from the Australian Hotel, right on the corner there. When he bought it ... when old Angelo bought it, he changed it into flats. He still lives there, but, all around, you see, it used to be a single man's quarters, like a boarding house. He sort of cut it up into flats and then he started renting them out and he started building it up. He was buying old houses around Bourke and he would rent them out. He would sell some and he would buy still more. Now, he owns half of Bourke; a very wealthy man, old Angelo. He knows how to look after a quid too. He does not like parting with it.

Getting back to New Park and the Cuffes: I used to go to Cunnamulla a fair bit, because, I was running a couple of girls up there at the time. I used to go with a girl called Evelyn Kirby and another one, Doreen Hooper. I thought about getting married and my old mate Chris he came up there again in winter '59, came back up roo shooting, him and Pat Simmons and Colin Gee. Because old Alec and Joy Cuffe knew that I was thinking about getting married, they decided to build another room – a bedroom and a kitchen and pantry onto the two-room hut that was already there. Colin Gee being a carpenter they got the job of doing it. We used to go to Cunnamulla, me and Chris and Pat and Colin; down to Enngonia. We used to go down there a bit. Yes, so anyway, I did get married, but not to either one of those girls.

I got married to Joanie McCarthy and ... I said that before actually. Anyway, Chris and them, they left after they finished building the house. I still worked at New Park. Then some other people came up from Sydney, these two detectives and one bloke that owned a second-hand car yard in Sydney. They got permission to come onto the place shooting. They wanted to shoot some pigs. There were a lot of pigs around then.

Billy Joins Forces with the Police and Visits Sydney Again

Anyway, old Alec Cuffe gave me permission to go with them and show them around, show them where all the tanks [ground tanks] were and were all the pigs were running. You know, the bore drains and things like that. Anyway, I got pretty friendly with these guys. This Detective Sergeant Rames, he invited me back down to Sydney, but that was a few years after. I think it was in '62 or '63, I am not sure. I went back down to Sydney and made it my business to go out and visit my old mate Chris at Bondi. I met his wife-to-be at that time when I went down, Virginia. He was not married then, but he was getting close. I beat him to the punch anyway. Yes, I stayed with the police bloke, me and another bloke that was working there with me, 'Cook' Ellwood, Ernie Ellwood is his name. He is related to me in a way. Anyway, he came with us. We drove down to Sydney. First time driving in the traffic. I had the Volkswagen. Old Fred and his wife and his two daughters came to Parramatta and met us at the Parramatta post office.

I followed him all the way into Liverpool to where he lived. That was a good trip that, because I'd teed it up. The other guy, Ted Lloyd, he was a detective as well. So they were working out of Lidcombe Police Station. Anyway, they invited us to go on the run with them at night, on patrol in the police car. It was a big Fairlane car, Four, they called it. It was one of the biggest, busiest cars in that area. Anyway, Cooker and I thought we were the ant's pants sitting up in this police car with these coppers and I can remember one car that we chased had eleven people in it and there was only one girl out of the whole lot that did not have a police record.

Those blokes, those detectives, they see somebody walking along the street and they never forget them. They know who they are and they say, 'Yes, I know this bloke. I had him in for something.' you know, they had a memory like an elephant. They never forget. Yes, it was about … I can remember we walked into this hamburger shop about 3 o'clock in the morning. At that time, it was a time when all the railway station safes were getting knocked off.

They were backing a tow truck and the tow truck had a boom on it and they used to back the truck in through the windows, or the doors, and hook the safe on and take it. It was at this time that this was happening in Sydney. Anyway, we came to this railway siding out in the suburbs. I forget where it was, but we were just driving around. We saw this car and they radioed in the licence plate and asked if it was stolen. It was stolen and we thought that we had these blokes that were knocking the safes off. Anyway, we all got out of the police car. We were walking around, sneaking around the side of this railway station. We thought we had them, but there was no one there, but somebody had left the car there. There was no one around. So I reckon, and even the police said that it could have been, they saw us coming and took off. It was really exciting to be out driving around with these big coppers.

I remember, I was going to say, we walked into this hamburger shop at 3 o'clock in the morning. The jukebox was up, you know, real loud, and the young kids were all dancing and jiving around the place. As soon as they saw the police … there was me and this other bloke, Dick Cox, he was a detective, a big man, red-headed fellow he was. Him and I walked in to get some coffee and hamburger. When they saw the police walk in, they all stopped and everybody sat down and it was real quiet.

I thought I was just 'it', you know, walking in with this big, copper. A blackfella from the bush and I thought it was really great. I will never forget it. It was a great experience. On that trip there, Ernie and I, we went out to Bondi and Chris and I and Cooker went down the beach. There was thousands of people. This one girl, I mean, bikinis were getting sort of pretty small. Anyway, Chris sung out in the lingo, because we understood, but we were embarrassed, because we knew what he said. We did not realise that we were the only ones that knew what he said, but there was a lot of people and we sort of got, well, a bit shamed actually, because what he had said. We were glad when we realised that no one else understood what he said anyway. Yes, that was a good trip that.

The Cuffes of New Park

Yes, when I got back from that trip there, the Cuffes were going away. They were going on a world cruise. It was on a P&O liner. Anyway, they went and old George, Alec's brother, he came there to New Park and there was a mob of sheep on the market, I can remember. Old George said to me, he said, 'Well, you're the boss. You count the sheep and give delivery of the sheep.' I knew how to count sheep and that, and argue the price, but I did not know that old George was sort of pushing me into doing it, you know? Because he reckoned that I was the boss and I was in charge; he was only caretaker. So he let me take the responsibility of delivering the sheep to these people by counting them over and, like that, to the stock and station agent. I remember that quite plain actually.

I got cards from the Cuffes and when they were over in the Philippines I got postcards from there. I got postcards from Honolulu. It was great getting all these cards from overseas, from the Cuffes. I remember when they came back. They were pretty good to me actually. They looked after me well. I can remember when they came back, because the old BSA rifle I had was wearing out. Old Alec bought this new French rifle back. The brand of the gun was a Unique.

There was a fight. I forget what title fight it was, but, there was a fight on. I was saying I wished I had a wireless so I could listen to this fight. Anyway, that night we finished work and I was sitting down at the hut and I heard this music and I did not know where the hell it was coming from. It was old Alec coming down the paddock and he had this little transistor behind his back. Anyway, he came down. It was for me. I got this transistor radio and the Unique rifle.

He pulled the Unique rifle out of the box and he said, 'Can you put it together?' It was in pieces, you know? Anyway, yes, I did. It took me a long time, but I finally got it together. There was this beautiful, big, travelling rug they brought back from over there somewhere. No, they were really good to me, those people. Yes, then I done and got married.

He was a hard, hard man to work for, yes. I mean, you had to work hard, but he … most times he was sticking there with you. I was only a young fellow and he was an old man, but he was brought up in a hard school, too. You know, like he would swing the old Kelly with you and he would use the crowbar, yes. But a fair man, very fair. He paid me over the award wage. He used to try and help me save and he used to give me sheepskins, and any dead wool around the place I picked up was mine. I would take it all into the shed and press it, put it into bales and then he would lend me the ute to take it into Cunnamulla and sell it to the skin shop.

He was good to me, really good, I think, because they did not have any kids. I think to myself, if I had stayed there, I probably would have finished up with a bit more. Anyway, we got on well, you know a few things happened towards the end and it was why I decided to leave.

Life after New Park

Joanie, when I married her, she already had two kids and the girl, Maureen, she was sort of getting onto school age. So we more or less had to leave and go into town so she could go to school. We started giving her correspondence, but, you know, a mother teaching her daughter did not really work very well. So anyway, we decided to go in and they started school in Bourke. Joanie and I worked … well, Joanie worked at the Royal at first, at the Royal Hotel [now the Port of Bourke Hotel] in Bourke. She was a waitress there on the tables. Then I was at the meatworks. Then she got a job at the meatworks as well because it was permanent and it was good money. Then her mother got sick and she went to Charleville. She flew to Charleville on the plane.

Her mother and her bloke came down and picked her up in Charleville from Winton. They took her to Winton. A couple of months after, I finished up and I flew to Longreach by plane and then I got the train from there across to Winton. This Darcy Cummins that Joanie's mother was living with, he had a taxi. So I bought into that with him. I worked in the sheds there for a while rouseabouting. I bought into the taxi with Darcy. It took me about two months to get my licence. When I applied for it, the police said I had already applied for it. So I could start driving straight away. So I did. That was the year Gatum Gatum won the Melbourne Cup [1963].

Finishing up I had the cab by myself. He took off and went to live in Rockhampton. We had the house and the taxicab. I worked that.

That was up in Winton. Darcy came back and he wanted his share of the cab, so we had to turn around and sell it. We got £400 for the plates. We just took the plates off and kept the car. We had a Holden station wagon. He had a Falcon Squire that he had bought because we had two contracts when we had the taxicab.[37] One was with the railway. We used to have to carry a gun, because, we used to have to go and pick up the payroll every second Wednesday.

We had licensed revolvers. We had to have a licence because we were carrying large sums of money and we had to go and pick the stationmaster up with the payroll. Instead of leaving it in the safe overnight we used to take it to the bank and they would bank it overnight. The next morning we would have to go and pick him up and take him down to get the brown leather bag that the money was in, and take it back to the railway. It was all pay packets; it used to come from Rockhampton. That was all right. We used to take that back and that was one contract we had.

The other contract we had was with the TAA. We used to have to go and pick the mailbags up and bring them into the post office. Then we would go back and clean the plane out. We would bring the crew in too; the crew and the pilot. They used to stay at the North Gregory Hotel. We used to have to go back and get all the cooking utensils, the plates and take them in. They would be washed by another woman and refuelled again, as I say, and go. We would stock them up with the food again and then we would take them back the next day. Then we would pick up the crew and take them back.

Blokes used to ring up from way out near Boulia, 200 miles, and he would ring up the cab because he would want to come into town for a few days, do some shopping and that. Yes, you used to go out, you know, miles. When you were driving the cab, you had to be dressed. I used to wear a white shirt and a tie. Going out into those places, the bulldust … and this ringer would ring up like 10 o'clock at night sometimes. You would get a phone call and you would have to go. You would sort of drive all night and get back the next day.

The bulldust out there was shocking because it was all out in the Diamantina, out in the flooded country. Big trucks and that, like road trains, yes, on those

---

37. The Falcon was used unofficially as a second taxi for a TAA (Trans Australian Airlines) contract.

roads. The big trailers cut the road up something terrible. It was good money. We used to make good money.

They used to call from down the reserve, the Aboriginal reserve. They used to call it the Boomerang Avenue, the reserve, and I had to go down and pick this bloke up so he could come up and put a bet on. We had just walked into the SP bookie and they [the police] jumped. I had £10 to put on Gatum Gatum and it won at 100 to 1. I was really spewing because I missed the bloody race.

Yes, up in Winton there when I had the cab, this bloke rung up one night, or one afternoon, and I had to go about 260 miles to this property and pick him up. I left Winton sort of late afternoon and by the time I got out there it was pretty late. It was daylight the next day, coming back. It was coming over this flooded country on the Diamantina. We were looking for a waterhole, to have a bit of a bogie because it was hot and with the dust and all that. I took another bloke with me, Johnny Anderson. He was Darcy's nephew. He came with me for the ride. We had this bloke in the car, this ringer. We decided to go for a bit of a walk down this bit of a channel so we could have a bogie and we saw these big tracks. I have seen plenty of tracks, like, I know a track when I see it. This track was too big for a goanna and I am sure it was a crocodile. I am absolutely sure it was because I have never seen a goanna that size. I said to Johnny, 'Well, bugger the water, mate, if this fellow is poking around here, you are not catching me going in the water.' So we suffered it out and jumped in the car and took off again.

Then when we sold the cab. Knowing the old stationmaster there fairly well, I mean, because of the times I had taken him to the bank and picked him up and picked the money up and things like that, anyway, I asked him for a job. He gave me a job as a porter on the railway. So I worked there for just a bit under twelve months, I suppose. We used to have to clean the train out. What do they call it? *The Inlander*, from Rockhampton.

We used to have to clean that out, all the ashtrays and the things and the toilet and showers and things like that. And empty all the rubbish bins and wipe all the seats down and clean it out and unload all the goods trains that used to come in there, because Winton was the end of the line from Rockhampton. That is the furthest it came and then it went back. I am sure the name of the train was *The Inlander*, a big, silver train. It had showers and sleepers and everything in it.

Moves to Rockhampton and Becomes a Part-Time Entertainer

Yes, then I worked there for a while. Then Darcy and Joanie's mother went to Rockhampton to live. So they wrote us letters. I used to sing a bit in those days and Darcy wanted me to go down because they had a band going in Rockhampton. Johnny and I used to do a lot of singing. So we decided to pack up and go. So we went to Rockhampton. I could not get a job there so I went back on the railway, but as a fettler. You know, like doing taxi driving, because it was no hard work and then working on the rail, being a porter, just cleaning the platform down and cleaning the trains and unloading the goods trains, there was no hard work attached to it. Then I got the job there as a fettler and had to go out and swing a crowbar and pick and shovel. I had blisters the first few days. All my hands came up in blisters. I suffered there for the first week.

There was a place called Edungalba about 50 miles out of Rockhampton. We used to go up to – there was a big mission not far from there – Duaringa, and a lot of blackfellas there. It was straight past the old Premier's property, what is his name? Bjelke-Petersen, yes. I can remember there one bloke, Willy Rowrow his name was, an Aboriginal bloke, and we mated it up with him, a really nice bloke. He had a car, so we used to get the train in. Joanie and I used to go in because they used to play this game they called cut 'em.[38] It was a card game and if you were lucky enough you could win a lot of money. We were pretty keen on the

---

38. Cut 'em is a card game in which each player cuts the pack in turn and the one with the highest card wins the hand.

game, both of us, so every payday we used to go in there for a night. Willie and his wife would bring us back.

On the road from Duaringa to Edungalba it was like dirt road and rough as anything, but old Joh's place, he had the bitumen right through to the homestead from the highway. I do not know how he did it, but being the premier of Queensland I suppose he carried a bit of weight. Yes, he was a cunning old fella, I think, old Joh. Yes, anyway, we worked there and then I was out of Edungalba and then Darcy came out. I used to go in like on the weekend.

Sometimes I would go in and sing with the band. Then I was waiting for a job at the meatworks, at the Lake Creek meatworks in Rockhampton. So, finally my name came up and Darcy brought the message out. So I made an excuse to leave the railway on a minute's notice to take this job at the Lake Creek meatworks. So I did anyway. I made an excuse and the bloke said, 'Well, you know, if you want to come back, you can always come back here.' So I went in there and I started working there, but they had so much trouble with the unions, that you know, you would work for two or three days and then they would strike for two or three days. It was no good to you.

Anyway, Darcy he got this big house and it was cut up into two flats and he rented the whole lot out. He had, like, me and Joanie were living there and Darcy and Joanie's mother, and then there was another bloke, Mickey Connellan and his wife and two kids. Plus the single blokes like Harry Hyles and Johnny Cummins, which was Darcy's nephew. Of course they were all in the band, see.

Micky was a good guitar player and a good piano player. Harry was a good guitar player and Johnny was a vocalist/guitarist and Darcy could play anything. He was really good. He couldn't sing, but he could play any instrument, like electric steel and just ordinary. He was the lead guitarist in the band, but he was really good and Johnny and I used to sing. I'd play bass sometimes, but, yeah, we used to work all round the pubs and the clubs and we used to … In the next street where we used to live there was a hall just down the street and Darcy used to rent that out every now and again and put on a dance for the black people.

Of course, Darcy'd get takings from the door and, well, supposed to halve it up with us, but never ever did, because we were paying rent and when they left … We used to give him the money for the rent and he used to go and gamble it, and then he was behind with the rent, so he took off and left Joanie and I there. Then Micky took off; the band split up. Micky took off and Harry went with Darcy and Joanie's mother to Brisbane. They moved to Brisbane, and unknowns [*sic*] to us they were behind with the rent and we didn't know, so the bloke came around and he said, 'Well, I want some rent,' and we said, 'We thought Darcy was paying you the rent, because we were paying him.'

To Brisbane

Anyway, it so happens that it was a couple of hundred quid and we didn't have the money to pay it. Bertie McCarthy, that's Joanie's brother, the young fellow, he was only about sixteen or seventeen, he had a little [money]. Well, at first we tried to hitch-hike to Brisbane, so we went out to the road and we tried to hitch-hike to Brisbane and couldn't get a ride.

So Bertie said, 'Well, I'll go and hock this transistor wireless' that he had, so the fare for the two of us one way was £8 16, so this bloke only wanted to give us six quid for the wireless so I talked him into … I said, 'Look, mate, we've got to get to Brisbane, it's important.' I said, 'We've got important business to do.' So anyway, I talked him in to giving us the bare £8.16, which was for the fare for the two of us. We got to Roma Street in Brisbane and then we walked from Brisbane to Hendra [approx. 11 km], right out where the stables were where Darby was living.

We had nothing to eat because we had no money. We walked right out to Hendra and we knew where Richard, or Darby, was staying and he wasn't at home so we waited there. Nearly all day we waited. He was away somewhere at a country meeting and, anyway, I went for a walk along the street. I had a few pennies in my pocket so I walked up to this little shop and I got a packet of lollies and was on my way back down to where we was waiting for Darby to come home and I saw the blue Zephyr drive past. He waved and as soon as I saw him I knew it was Darby, and I said, 'Hey, come here I want to see you, mate.'

And anyway, he said, 'Oh, Billy, I didn't recognise you.' So, anyway, we jumped in the car and he took us for a big feed. We had a feed and I had to borrow the money off him to go back and pay this bloke the rent because we got, you know, put in an awkward position there. Anyway, he lent me the money and shouted a feed and paid our night in the hotel. He booked us into a hotel and paid for that for us and gave us the money to go back. Then we moved to Brisbane as well. We came down there and I started working at a tin factory, pressing tin.

That was in '65. I think it was '65. Yeah, I worked there for a while and then it was too hard to bend those big … I was only a little light fella then and I couldn't lift the big square pieces of tin. We used to press it together with a press and it was too heavy. I was there for a few weeks, but I couldn't, you know … It was a bit too heavy for me, so I decided to give these drilling rigs a go. They were working out at Tara and Joanie's youngest sister, she was living with Johnny Troutman and he said, 'Come out.' He said, 'You might have to wait a few days,' he said, 'to get on, but you will eventually get on because people are coming and going all the time.'

Anyway, the rail motor used to go from Brisbane out to Tara and so I jumped on the rail motor, because Johnny Troutman, he was working for the Americans there on these drilling rigs. So, anyway, I went out there and I waited. I was there three days, four days, and they came around at 4 o'clock in the morning to pick me up to go to work, and I started work. Boy oh boy, she was hard yakka! I mean, those blokes, I mean when they started work, you started at, sort of 5 o'clock, and you worked till 7, 8, 9, 10 o'clock at night.

We were looking for oil. I was off-siding. I started off-siding, just shovelling dirt and changing the drilling rods on the rigs and all my fingers swelled up and my wrists swelled up and I didn't have the proper clothes. I had R.M. Williams riding boots on and then I finally got my first pay; I had no money. I got my first pay, but had to go out to Toowoomba to pick it up, and I got my pay and I went and bought myself a pair of gumboots and the right sort of gear for the job. I stayed with them for, nearly two years, I suppose.

Joan and I were, sort of, having problems at the time. We were still together, but, you know, we were having a few problems, but she came out to Tara. She was out at Tara.

Domestic problems, you know. Because I started drinking then, too, and Joan was drinking, like, and we was having problems, so we decided to, sort of, call it quits. I think most of the problem was … I mean, we were trying very hard to have kids, but we couldn't succeed in that, and I think that was most of the problem. But, anyway, we sort of parted, as friends, and she went her way and I went my way. It was 1982, I think, when my divorce was finalised.

We drove the rigs down to Brisbane when we finished our contract all out around Tara and St George, Surat, Miles. We done the pipeline from Moonie where they struck the oil. We done the pipeline from there into Ipswich putting in anode beds to check the corrosion on the pipeline because they'd fly it every day to check for leaks and that.

Anode beds, they'd call them. We used to drill like 200–300 foot [61–92 m] alongside of the pipeline every so many miles and put in these … they were wrapped in that stuff you get in the torch battery. It's sort of black on the outside and it's got this piece of black stuff in the middle, so it was like that but only ten times bigger. We used to put that in and pack it in coke and it had electric cable on it. The electric cable had to go down the hole in this stuff and then we welded it on to the pipeline, and it had a red and black disc.

The way it worked, if there was a leak in that section of the line the black disc would move and it showed the red behind it, and that way the plane would pick it up when the plane would fly over it. If there was a leak in that section, well, the plane would radio straight into base and then they'd send a crew out to fix it up. It was only the air checks like, if it was rusting or if there was a leak or something like that, like, bad condition. I don't understand it, but we had two engineers working with us and they'd tell us what to do and we'd do it.

In some places it would run along the top of the ground. In other places it would be down, probably five, six foot underground.

That took us almost twelve months to do that job. We finished that and we went to Rocklea in Brisbane and there was a crew … Well, I was going to go to Madagascar, actually, in Africa, but Ray Leek, a mate of mine, he was on another crew and he got there before me and he put in for the job too, and he beat me to it. So he went to Madagascar and they knew I wanted to go overseas so they offered me a job in New Guinea. They showed me a video clip of New Guinea and the conditions where you're working in the jungle with water up to your waist and these blackfellas were swimming around with the crocodiles and I said, 'Well, *this* blackfella won't be going over there.' So, they gave me a choice then to go to Melbourne. So I went to Melbourne instead and we worked down there. I was, sort of, drilling offsider, and we were down there for about twelve months. It was when the [water] restrictions were on in Melbourne and we were doing mostly golf courses and hospitals and bowling greens and market gardens, or people with money that wanted water.

We went down there in '67, I think it was. We left there in '68. It was close to Christmas actually and Phil Wayne and myself and his wife …

We were working for United Geophysics, but it was different work. You see, we were doing oil exploration in Queensland and we were doing water bores in Victoria. All out around Echuca, Rochester, Bendigo, all those places, right down as far as Foster in Wilsons Promontory. We went right down to there. A place called Squeaky Bay I can remember.

Central New South Wales and Romance

Yeah, then we heard about the big overtime money that they were getting with the Water Conservation/Irrigation Commission in Dubbo.

It's now called Water Resources but back in those days it was WC&IC and we heard about that because some of the boys that used to work for United they went to the Commission and they were working there. One bloke, an old Pommy bloke, Jim Evans he came back to United and he was telling us about the big money that you could make if you wanted to work overtime. See, so of course everybody was screaming for water and the Water Commission, they first bought these Mayhew 1000 rigs, and they didn't know how to operate them so Phil and I put in for the job and we got it.

Phil Wayne came from Wyandra in Queensland. So, him and I put in for … He wrote away for the job, like, for both of us. They had no kids; they were just a young married couple, so we left there and I went with them. They had their own car and caravan and we got the job there. We came up to Dubbo and started work there and that's where I met the wife of all my kids. She was a white woman – Val, Valerie Grant – and we was together for thirteen years, almost thirteen years.

They lived out at a little village just out of Dubbo called Mogriguy and we done a water bore at Eumungerie, which was only a few miles up the track, in between Gilgandra and Dubbo. Yeah, we drilled a water bore there for the school and, of course, they had a little pub there at Eumungerie and after work we used to go over there and, of course, having a guitar and singing songs and that, well, back in those days everybody enjoyed it, your know. So, I saw this blonde sheila in the pub and her mother, actually, was the one that came over and asked me to play 'Mona Lisa'. And, anyway, I done 'Mona Lisa' and then the girl came over and sort of introduced herself and said, 'Do you know such and such?'

And anyway, that was the, sort of, beginning of my married life for the second time. Yeah, we finished up at a party that night, over the creek out of Eumungerie. It was in between Eumungerie and Mogriguy where she lived, and Coolbaggie Creek they used to call it, so a big mob of people finished up out there after the pub closed and we had a big fire, and a big singsong around the fire. Yeah, so anyway, I started going with her and I was still working away and then the Commission gave me my own rig. I was driller in charge of the crew and I was shifted to Werris Creek up near Tamworth.

I done all the observation work in the Mooki Valley. I was there for five years in that valley. I done all the drilling all around Werris Creek, the Breeza Plains, up to Narrabri; from Narrabri, Wee Waa and just doing observation bores.

It was only just testing the how much the irrigation and the bores were taking out of the table, out of the water table, because, you see, you have got to have a licence to put down a water bore and if they thought that there was too many bores in the one area they wouldn't let drillers in there, you see. They wouldn't give the cockies a licence to put down a water bore [if the level was low]. That was my job doing that.

I bought a house in Werris Creek. I had life insurances going and I cancelled all them to buy my house and that's how I got my house. Bought my house and I worked for the Commission for almost eight years and we had four kids. Well, Val had two kids to a previous marriage, a boy and a girl, and then I'd fathered four at that time. We had four kids and then we went to … We were living in Werris Creek there for quite a few years and in 1974 there was a job advertised in Western Australia, because I was going away a lot then, you know.

It was all right when I was in the Mooki Valley because I did not have to camp out. But shifting up to Narrabri and Wee Waa when I was living away through the week, and only coming home sometimes. We'd have to work Saturday and

I'd only get home for Saturday night and then I'd leave again Sunday night to go back to work and that wasn't doing us any good. Then this job was advertised in Western Australia up in the Hamersley Ranges at a place called Paraburdoo and Tom Price. Up in that area, 1000 miles [1600 km] north of Perth, and they were advertising for married drillers, so I applied for the job and went to Sydney for the interview.

Drilling in Western Australia

We got the job and moved over there in 1974. It took me a week, because the Nullarbor wasn't tarred. It was all dirt and it took me a week to get to Perth from Dubbo and all my kids, like, the six kids and the caravan. I had an old Valiant station wagon, an old 318 V8, a great old car. It took us all the way and we had one puncture. The caravan was, you know, too much weight in it, because we had to shift so much We sold our house, sold all our furniture, but we had all the clothes and, like, cooking utensils, and the kids' toys and all that sort of stuff. But we went up there in '74 and left in 1980, yes September. The end of September 1980 I left there. Yeah, Val and I had split up when we were working up there and she moved to live in Perth.

Well, she was playing up on me because, like being a shift worker and she was, sort of, pretty lonely at home, I suppose, I don't know. So I suggested she join the women's dart club. It was the worst thing I ever done in my life, because they used to play in the pub, you see. Of course, me at work and she had the free leg to go to the pub and play and then, I mean, there's like, 400 single blokes there in the town. A lot of single blokes and very few women, so it wasn't very hard.

It was my stepdaughter actually. She let the cat out of the bag. I put it to her, I said, 'Well, what's going on?' and she said, 'Well, look I've got to tell you, Dad,' she said, 'Mum's playing up on you.' So, I just started – asked her [Val] why she wouldn't tell me before and why I had to find out from Gina. Oh, it sent me silly, mate. It put me in hospital for three days, but I got out of that and she moved to

Perth. Being on a four-shift roster we used to get about five days off every three weeks, so I used to fly down to Perth and see my kids when they were living in Perth there because she used to … She got tangled up with a local Aboriginal at a suburb called Girrawheen in Perth and Gina was only about, I don't know, very young, in her young teens.

She was the oldest, yes. Val ended up putting Gina in the girl's home so when I came down I said, 'Well, where's Gina?' and she said, 'Well, I put her in the home because I couldn't handle her.' This is what Val told me. Then I found out why she put her in there, because she couldn't have the free leg, because Gina used to go crook on her, see, about having blokes in the house. So, I went out and I got Gina out of the home and I took her back to Paraburdoo with me and she was up there with me for a while and then she went back. I put her on the plane and sent her back down to Perth. She wanted to go back. She landed there and went home and there was a bloke in the house with her mother, so she wanted to come straight back to Paraburdoo again and I couldn't afford to just fly her round, you know, like that.

So on my next break I went down and I was leaving again to go back. I bought another car, a Fairlane, and my little boy, my baby fella [Clayton], he was only about three year old, and he started to cry and, you know, get upset because I was going away again, so I just kicked the door in and walked in the house and grabbed all the clothes and threw them and the suitcase in and I said, 'I'm taking my kids.' So I took all the kids, barring Gina. I took all the other kids, even her boy, David, took them all back to Paraburdoo with me. It used to take us a couple of days, like, to drive 1000 miles, because there was only a bit of dirt so it was a pretty good road. From Nanuttara [Roadhouse] into Paraburdoo was about 160, 170 miles [approx. 260 km] that was dirt, but it's all tar now. But then a week later she followed us back. She came back up there and I was paying her maintenance and that and she wasn't giving the kids what they were supposed to be getting out of the money. So she came back up to Paraburdoo and we were only there a week, because previous to that I'd put in for a job in South America, and I found out a week after I went back that I got the job.

It was with Western Geophysical, one of the biggest exploration companies in the world, based in Houston, Texas.

Billy operating drilling rig, Paraburdoo, WA, 1977/78.

Up in Paraburdoo I was just finishing nightshift, out there. I was on nightshift, and one of the trucks tipped ... you see they used to carry about 200 ton. They had big haul packs and iron ore that they carried. In one area the boulders were too big and the truck backed up to the crusher. They used to tip it down into the crusher and it jammed the mantle, and they had to swing a little air track on the crane. They've got an overhead crane there to put the pulleys down with a hook on it to pull the rocks out and then hit them with the crusher to crush them up.

But this one was too big so it jammed and, anyway, it was my job, I had to go down into the crusher and drill a few holes with the air track to put the explosives in to blow it up, because you couldn't get it out, it was jammed solid, you see, so the only way you could do it was to break it up. You'd have to go down and drill a couple of holes and put a half a stick of jelly in it and then blow it. Well, then it would break it up and free the crusher.

Anyway, I was doing that and it was so bad that, like, swinging with the harness. I had a safety harness on and swinging on the end of this rig and I was, like, reversing and forwarding and reversing the rig, like the bit, and the thing unscrewed and I had a bent rod on so that I could work in the dirt more to try and free this boulder and it started to undo because of the pressure on one side. A piece of thread come off and went straight through my eye and that's how it buggered my eye up and I went to Perth. I was in hospital in Perth for about seven weeks and about three operations later, yeah. You see it [the boulder] was too big to go through the crusher and, of course, the trucks didn't know it was down there. They kept tipping and it was too late. Like, two or three trucks with 400 ton of iron ore down in the crusher. I mean, the crusher was a great big bowl, you know, like a big bowl. Like the mantle on a Tilley light.[39]

Well, the crusher was the shape of that down in the middle and it used to vibrate and the stones would fall through and it would crush them up small and they'd go on to a belt, a conveyer belt, and take it out to the stockpile. [The control room was above the crusher.] They're all electric with some hydraulics. It looks like a cockpit in an aeroplane, but twice as big, like, all the electric things that operate this crusher. You've got two blokes in there, a push-button job and you're sitting there and you push a button to start it and stop it and to crush; to start your conveyer belts and all your blowers and all that sort of thing. Very interesting.

Yeah, but that's how it happened. Anyway, I got that job overseas and then I said to Val, I said, 'Do you want to stay in Perth or do you want to go back to Dubbo?' See, she come from Dubbo originally. And she said, 'No, we'll go home,' so I shifted them all back to Dubbo and I had to take off overseas.

Billy, Val and children near Dubbo, 1980. Billy left for Ecuador shortly after this photo was taken.

---

39. A Tilley light is a portable kerosene lantern. By means of pumping the kerosene in the container at the bottom of the lantern the liquid is pressurised and fed though a hydro-pneumatic blowpipe to the mantle, which provides the light when lit. The term has also become a generic term for other kerosene lanterns.

PART TWO

… any boy that's worth his salt will roll his swag and roam

– Banjo Paterson

South America – Ecuador

Yes going back to that job in South America: it was advertised in the *Western Australian* paper, so I applied for it and I go the job. I went over there as a driller for oil exploration, and it so happened there was another Australian there when I got there. I started on night shift and I couldn't speak a word of Spanish, and I had all Ecuadorian offsiders, and buggy drivers, to cart the water.

I had a rough time. The first night was pretty rough and then I started to pick up a little bit here and there. About three months and I could sort of speak fairly good Spanish, but it was pretty rough there for a while. I was only drilling for not quite three months actually, and then they made me a supervisor, and then I started looking after the rigs. I had 24 rigs, and about 300 men scattered all over the place. Used to travel around in a helicopter. In the jungle, like the terrain was so bad that they used to send a crew in just to blaze a trail, just enough to walk along. This was for the portable rigs. On the flat country we used to use the buggies, four-wheel-drive buggies

The crew was called a trocha crew. I'd say it was Spanish, yes, trocha [path/track]. They'd go in and clear just enough so you could walk along [about 2.4 m in width]. Some of the places there … they used to make ladders out of the timber there in the jungle. They'd make ladders so you could go up the side of a cliff. On the seismic crew, when they peg a line, you go straight, no matter what's in front. If it's a cliff, if it's a river, you still go straight. Anyway, that started in Ecuador, the job.

Billy in Ecuador, waving from a helicopter.

But, leaving Australia was … I didn't really want to go. When I got the job, I was excited about having the job, but when the time came to go I sort of, you know, my kids were there and I didn't like leaving them behind, but anyway, I did get away. Before I went, I had to go and have injections for typhoid and cholera, and a couple of other things you needed to get to go over into those countries. I broke out in all these sores around my lip, all cold sores, and it was in October, and I was freezing in the mid-summer. I was covered over with blankets. The needles made me terrible crook.

I didn't even have an interview for the job. When I told them what I'd done, what sort of work I'd done over the years, like, I was drilling for twenty-something odd years then, 23 or 25 years or something.

The interview was by phone, from Paraburdoo to Houston, Texas. I spoke to Mr Vic Boyd at first. He was one of the bosses. The other guy, I forget his name, the bloke that actually gave me the job. They must have talked it over. Anyway, I got the job.

I flew from Dubbo to Sydney and then from Sydney to Los Angeles. The first stop was Honolulu, and then the next stop was LA, and the next stop was Bogota in South America. The next stop was Quito, in Ecuador. I got there and I was tired, because of the jet lag. I wasn't used to those sort of trips on a plane. When I got to Honolulu I can remember, because I had all these sores around my mouth and I was a bit embarrassed about it, I couldn't cover them over.

They sort of come on me going across, but it was only the after-effects from the injections I had. I'd ask somebody where to go, like these big Negro blokes there, and they, you know – sort of because I think you were a foreigner – they weren't very helpful anyway, some of them. Some of them were but ... that's in Honolulu.

Then I got to Colombia and Ecuador, and I booked in. Everything was booked ahead for me, and I jumped in a taxi. I had US dollars that I got in Sydney before I left and I wasn't aware of the currency in Ecuador. When we got to the hotel they had me booked into, the taxi driver was speaking in Spanish. Well, I didn't know what he was talking about, but he was telling me how much it was. So I thought, well back home this would cost about $1, so I gave him $1 and he was quite happy with that. It was close enough to what he was talking about, because when he saw the US dollars he was quite happy.

Murray Morrel from Calgary, Canada, and Billy with skin from a boa constrictor. The skin had been cut in half lengthways. Base camp, East Ecuador, 1981.

Billy with his captain (also translator) and his cook, Ecuador.

So anyway, I found out later on, when I learned a bit of Spanish, he was saying treinta, which meant 30 sucres, and one US dollar was 36 sucres, so he got a little bit more than he bargained for. Anyway, I went, I went in the office there and the bloke that was running the show, he was Australian, Dieter, his name was, Dieter Myles. He'd lived in South America for quite a few years. He married an American woman and they had a farm, or plantation, in Ecuador. Anyway, he was the boss, so he told the area supervisor to send me to a place called Puna. It was an island and I had to travel to another town, or a city, called Guayaquil.

Well, we left Guayaquil at 4 o'clock in the morning. We travelled all day and into the night, because we got caught, because of the tide. They misjudged the tide, because usually they'd time it so they got to the island on a high tide, so you could get right into the wharf. But we were stranded out in the mudflats there for a while, out in the mangroves. High and dry. I mean, there was still water there, but the boat bottomed and couldn't move off. We had to wait there for the tide to come in, so we could get into the place. Yes, but anyway, we got there and it was early hours of the morning. I had a couple of blokes there, carrying my suitcases up to the tent. We were living in tents and, anyway, next morning they sung out to me about 5 o'clock, I only had a couple of hours sleep, and had to go out into the fly camps, right out in the jungle.

We had tents out there too. Well, fly camp was a name that, like, it had a base camp and a fly camp. The base camp was a base, but you had two-way radios and this was when I was drilling, and when I started supervising. Well mostly I'd be in base camp, but used to travel around wherever I could in the ute, to the camps and in the helicopter.

War broke when we was there, too, Peru against Ecuador. I went out to put all my blokes to work and they were all gone, they went to the war. Only lasted three days, but they only left some of the old blokes there, and I was saying, 'Where's all the men? They've got to go to work,' and they said, 'Oh, they're all gone to the war.' It lasted three days, but we had planes flying over the island and, yes, it was a bit scary there, because a couple of blokes that were in the camp, one bloke in particular, came from South Australia. His wife and two kids were in Ecuador and he was scared because, you know, it came to shots there in

Ecuador. The sirens were going and, because she was scared, she wanted him to come back in.[40]

We had a Peruvian there with us, on the island, see, and the military knew that; the Ecuadorian military knew. Anyway, they had to smuggle him out in the helicopter. He got out of it, and when everything settled down he came back, because he was one of the observers. You know, he had a pretty responsible job.

After three months I started supervising.

I had heaps of blokes under me, heaps of blokes. We had six buggies and there was probably about twelve, about twelve men to a buggy, because their wages were about 100 [US$] and the top men would be on about $200 a month, the most experienced ones. You'd pick them out, and it was our job to get the job done and then teach these blokes how to work the machinery. But you'd pick the most intelligent one out and then you'd sort of spend more time, you know, and teaching him the ropes, and teach him to operate the machinery. But we had six buggies and we had pack drills scattered all over the place.

There probably would have been about 300 men, I suppose, all local blokes, most of them. A lot of them from up in the Oriental, up in a place called Piuru. One crew there we had, one trocha crew and one drill crew, they were all Quechua Indians. They were Quechua Indians, right up from in the Amazon jungle. They were good workers, hard workers, and yeah, they … I went out with them blokes, actually. When we finished the contract on Puna, we got shifted to a place called Chone and we were working out of Chone. We had a contract there to do. There was one place there I went out with these blokes and camped with them, but they looked after me fairly well, because we had no transport and we had to walk and we were in the jungle.

I mean, it's a bit scary and I was by myself, but they looked after me fairly well. I think a lot of the other boys were a bit, sort of a bit scared to go out with them and camp with them like I did, because I was under the same [conditions]. Usually, you know, you've got your own cook and your own camp, but this time I went out because they were having trouble there getting water [to free the drills], and I just took my swag and an esky full of tucker and I shared it with them and they made me a bed out of bamboo. They were all sleeping on the ground.

---

40. The territorial dispute between Ecuador and Peru has been a long-running disagreement over the countries' borders.

The other people like me, like the Australians and the Pommies and the Kiwis and Americans, they were scared to live with these Quechua Indians. I mean, if they took a dislike to you they might just cut you up and no one would find you. Yes, the Quechua Indians, they were a lot different to the local boys there. Most of them came from Guayaquil, but there were villages on the island and we had a lot of workers from the villages. These Quechua Indians, especially the cooks, most of them were sort of in their forties, fifties, and when they'd go on a break they'd go into Guayaquil or go back to wherever they lived, and when they'd come back into camp they'd get a young boy, you know, probably nine, ten, eleven year old from Guayaquil. Because there were so many kids on the street, with no parents, and they'd do anything for a few bucks and a decent feed. So these blokes used to, these cooks, the Indians, they used to bring them back into the camp and just use the boys for their pleasure. I come across one once, and I fired him on the spot, but, you know, the poor little kids, I mean they're only doing it for survival. Yeah, to get out of the [situation] of what they were living in. Like, they were starving with no mother and father.

Another time there in Guayaquil I was going to meet the boat to go back to the island and I saw this little girl. She was about probably eight or nine. She had one little kid strapped in a piece of cloth over her shoulder, and another little one toddling alongside and she was looking in the garbage cans. So I pulled my driver up and I gave them some money to buy some food, but they were scraping the bottom of the garbage cans, and my driver said, 'Well, you know, you can't help them all, because there's so many.' I realised it was right what he was saying, but it just looked so terrible and I was thinking about my kids at home, and these little kids here just trying to survive on scraps. It was just unreal.

So, we went to Chone and we had a really good camp in Chone. The wet was just starting. They had a crew there before we went there. They had a carpenter crew there building the camp and all the camp was built out of, like it was built two feet from the ground, and it was all bamboo walks, bamboo floors for the tents and the kitchen and dining room area and office. It was all built, like it had corrugated iron on the top and bamboo walls. But it was a really nice camp.

The bamboo was about probably four to five inches around [100–125 mm in diameter]. Well, they used to go out and cut this bamboo and they'd bring it back to camp, and they'd split the bamboo and lay it out flat, and split it with machetes. They'd finish up with a wide piece, probably about eight or more inches wide and they'd use that for the walls. They'd just cut the bamboo down the middle just to open it out and flatten it and then they'd just tack that onto the wall. You know, they were good tradesmen; they knew their job.

The weather was very humid. In the wet season it was very humid with a lot of rain, but the water was no good. We had to drill our own water bore and that was my job. I'd drill the water bore for the camp. We had septic toilets and everything there, in that camp. It was really good because it was on the edge of town, see. It was funny though, when we'd go in and do any shopping, like go in to get parts, or something for the engines and that we'd go into Chone, and me being dark and looking like the natives there from their country, and they thought I was Ecuadorian. They'd look at me and they'd speak in Spanish, and it was just lucky enough that I knew what they were talking about and I wouldn't say anything, I'd just nod my head.

Anyway, all the boys there, one, this Ray Goodwin, he was a white bloke from Brisbane. He worked for United too, the other company that I worked for. Anyway, they'd look at one another and laugh, and the other fellow was Gary Reid, he came from South Australia, Adelaide. He was one of the observers there in the crew. Anyway, they'd laugh at these blokes. Like, they wouldn't talk to the whitefellas but they'd talk to me.

When we turned around to leave, I'd say to them in English I'd say, 'Thanks very much,' you know; 'it was nice knowing you,' or, 'it was good doing business with you.' Their mouth would fall open and their eyes would pop out of their head, because they didn't know I was Aboriginal. They thought I was a local boy. It was unreal.

Yeah, when we got onto the mainland, well – we had guards on the island as well – what they used to do, the local people, they'd follow you along like, we didn't know, but they'd sort of sneak along behind you. Because we used to load the holes, as we drilled them, we used to load them with explosives. Like a 60 foot hole would have five pound [about 2 kg] of explosives in it. What the blokes used to do, if they could pull it out they used to pull it out and just use the primer and one can of powder, because it was all screwed together, see.

They had the detonator and the primer and the can of powder, and they used to go to the creeks and fish with it. Well, we didn't know this was going on, until the shooter came along, like behind us, and the shooters would come along with the recorder to record the shots, and they used to find out some of the holes weren't loaded. And nine times out of ten we'd have to send a rig back there to clean the holes out and then put more powder in them.

Yeah, all the explosives were in cans, about the size of a Coke can. They screwed together and there was one on the top called the primer. It had a hole in the top of it and the detonator used to fit into the hole. Then there was another thing, a little plastic thing used to screw on the top to make sure the det [detonator] wouldn't come out. They were electric, you know, they used to hit them on the battery – put them on the battery – and then they'd go off, bang. But these guys were going around pinching the stuff and then we had to put guards on the lines, like, if it was close to a village. We used to put guards on the lines so they wouldn't go along and pull the explosives out.

There was one kid, a 14-year-old boy, he got a det and he was, I don't know, he was probably trying to find out how it worked, but he put it on a stone and he hit it and it took a bit of his finger, a bit of his thumb and half of his index finger, and a bit of the next finger … off his hand, but the company kept that quiet. They paid them. Paid them big, a big amount of money. When I say a big amount of money, they probably would have got a couple of grand out of it. Well, a couple of grand to them, that's nearly like $100,000 to us.

Most times if you were out in the, like walking, like we used to do, and carry the powder, we used to screw it together and probably carry a couple of sticks each. Like cans of powder are probably about, they would be four feet long [about 1200 mm], and we'd probably carry two or three or them each. But then they started to pinch it, and we found out what they were doing with it; they were fishing with it. They weren't stupid. They knew, you know, like them old blokes knew, anyway. There were crews there before, and whether they showed them how to do it or not I don't know. Yes, we had to have guards, even in the base camp in Chone. We had to have guards walking around there all night too, because they had the bodega [storeroom], what they called the bodega, and that was where all the food, like stores and spares parts and all that stuff was kept. Like, even us, if we had to get a part, we had to sign for it.

The guards had machine guns, but they were there 24 hours. I mean, you had them wandering around there in daytime, because some of the boys would slip in and pinch something. They were very light-fingered, but they, you know, on the whole I got along well with them, because being the same colour as them. Some of them were very keen to learn English, as keen as I was to learn Spanish.

Anyway, we finished Chone and we went to Quito, and all the crews got split up.

We'd been there six months in the highland, and about [inaudible] months in Chone, and when we left, like everything was auctioned, like, all your pots and pans, all your corrugated iron off the roof, all the office tables and chairs and all that sort of stuff was all sold.

The rigs weren't sold. We'd ship all the rigs; take all the rigs. It got shifted to a bodega in Quito, and all the boys were split up. Gary Reid and his wife, they went to Rio. I wanted to get to Rio something bad, but they had a full crew and I couldn't go, so they gave me a job looking after the bodega and the carpenters in Quito. We had to make all the wooden crates to ship all the parts, see, we were going to Venezuela by road, and all the motors and all the spare parts and the stuff like that had to be packed into crates.

So, I had a couple of carpenters just making these big crates. It was my job to look after them and answer the phone and pay them and buy them supplies and stuff like that. I'd go up to the office in Quito and they'd give me, sort of, $10,000 in local currency, and I used to carry this in a briefcase. This one day there I remember; I thought it was quite a classic, actually.

I was coming back from the bodega, it was only a walk to my hotel where I was living, and I had the black umbrella and the briefcase. I'm walking down the street and I had a little cackle to myself, and I'm thinking, 'If the fellas back home could see me now!' Like, if all my sisters and relations and that could see me walking along the street with this briefcase full of money and a big black umbrella.

I always wore my R.M. Williams boots and my jeans, and my old Akubra hat over there, yes.

R&R in Manta – Discrimination – Student Sex Workers

They treated me well. I mean, they treated me like a king. You know, the white people and … there was one bloke … we went to Manta. It was my break. I was working pretty hard, because you work sort of fifteen, sixteen, seventeen hours a day, seven days a week. You'd go home to go to bed and they'd come and wake you up at 3 o'clock, you'd have to get up and go again. But, you know, you got paid for it. We were getting good money, big money.

Anyway, they decided, because I was getting a bit cranky and I'd had enough for a while there, they said, 'Go for a couple of days break, or three or four days break.' They bought me a ute, a brand spanking new Toyota Hi-Ace, and they said, 'Get a driver to take you somewhere and leave you and then come back and pick you up.' So anyway, I got my driver to take me to a place called Manta, it was over on the coast from Chone.

Some of the boys had been there previous and they knew what it was like. And there was a couple of blokes I met. One was an American bloke. He got into the country with a fair bit of money and bought himself a banana plantation, pineapple plantation. He also bought himself a cathouse. You know, for the girls. Yes, a brothel. Anyway, we mated up with him and there was a bloke there, he came into the place on a ship, he was an American bloke, American Negro. They wouldn't let his ship go, for some reason or other, or something to do with the Customs. But anyway, he was caught then, he was there for over twelve months this bloke and he couldn't get out of the place. They wouldn't let him go and, anyway, they sort of mated up, you know, and there was about three or four of these blokes. One of them was a Colombian, one was an American Negro, and the other bloke was American, no, two Colombians, there was.

This bloke, this American, said to me, 'Do you want to come back to my place,' he said, 'and have a drink?' I thought this Negro bloke was coming with us, and when we got in the ute, like, this American bloke, he had a ute, or pick-up they call them over there, and I sort of moved over into the middle, and I thought this bloke was coming with us, this Negro bloke. I said, 'Well,' and then the bloke sort of took off and I said, 'Ain't he coming?' you know, this blackfella. And he said, 'No,' he said, 'I wouldn't have a nigger in my house.' And I was thinking about myself, like, back home I'd be classed as a, you know, nigger, or whatever. I thought, 'Gee whiz, this is strange,' like him being an American. Both American, one black and one white, but he was racialist, this bloke. It made me feel uncomfortable. I felt sorry for this poor, this poor bugger, because we went to the pictures, together, all of us, and he sat with us in the movies. And yeah, I was quite surprised when he came out with this, 'No,' he said, 'I won't have a nigger in my house.' But it was a funny thing, when we went back to his house and he went out to this place that he owned. I didn't know he owned it, but we went out there and he got these two girls from there and bought them back to his house, one of them was just like an American Negro. She was black, black as the ace of spades, and the other one was light, like me.

Yes, but it was funny, this place, because next day we went back to his joint, where we took the girls back to, and walked in, and the bloke there that was looking after the place, he run out with a cloth and he wiped the seats and he wiped the table, and he was calling this Roy, I forget his surname, but his name was Roy, and they were calling him Jefe. Well, Jefe means boss, see, and in Spanish, they were calling him Jefe. It sort of clicked, you know, this bloke here's the boss, he must own this joint. And I asked him, and he said, 'Yeah, I bought this place. I own it.' Yeah, it was unreal.

I mean all the rooms, all the schoolkids there, high-school kids, they were working their way through school. We went back there a couple of times, and once there in the afternoon, after the kids came out of school, I saw these girls about sixteen, seventeen, coming into the place, you know, in school uniform; and all the boys in their uniforms, like blue shirt and tie and that, and grey trousers, and I thought, 'Gee, what's going on here?'

All the rooms – they had a big line of rooms – looked like a stable to look at, and they had prices on top of the doors, how much it was to go and have … sleep with this girl for just half an hour or twenty minutes or so. Anyway, the popular ones had all these boys lining up and they all had, you know, their money in their hands, and they were all lining up, waiting to go in.

And some of the girls, like, seventeen, they were really pretty girls and they'd walk in a room in their uniform, and they'd come out with a towel wrapped around themselves and they'd parade around there for a while, and then they'd go back in and the boys would sort of line up, you know, but they were doing this to work their way through high school. They were getting money like this for their education, yeah. It was the only way they knew how.

I mean, they couldn't get a job, so they had to do it like that. Out there there was a lot of, well they call them ranches over there, and a lot of them were sort of pretty wealthy people. There's only two classes of people over there – you are either very rich or very poor. No middle class. And these boys, see, a lot of them were sent there, and even some of the girls were sent there, and I mean the wealthy, the real wealthy ones were all right, but some of them needed extra money and that's what they used to do.

The boys'd just go in there because the boys had money, because their parents owned the ranches around the countryside. It was only a country town, Manta was. I think, gee, I don't know how big it would be, but it wasn't that big, probably about 5000, 6000 people in it. Well, it might have been a bit more than that, it might have been 8000, 10,000 people, but it wasn't very big. It wasn't a big city. It was like a big country town.

We shifted back to Quito, like, after the Chone contract, and I was there for about three months. We were packing all the stuff up, ready to transport it to Venezuela. It was an experience and a half to travel from there, because we went through two borders. The first border was from Ecuador to Colombia, and then from Colombia to Venezuela, and everything went by trucks. All the rigs, you know, went on trucks.

Colombia to Venezuela – Corruption

It was a big convoy, mate. I mean, you can imagine all the rigs, and the only thing we did not take was all our utes. We had seven utes and we drove them to the border – to the Ecuador/Colombian border – and we left them there, and they left a bloke there with them to look after them. But, see, the company, instead of taking stuff out of the country, because it was so hard to get it back in, they used to use the stuff there and then put it in storage if they got another contract. Which was, you know, I mean it must have cost thousands and thousands of dollars. But anyway, we got to the Colombian border, then we left all the utes there. There was seven utes we had. Pick-ups they call them over there; Toyotas and that. We moved into Colombia and we were camped there for about three weeks, because, see, they all want money, and all these Custom officers and that, they sort of try and stall you. Because they were big companies, they knew that if they stalled them long enough, they'd get paid something. Anyway, they'd sort of negotiate and come to terms, and then they'd say, 'No,' and they'd be hanging off for more money and all that sort of thing until the company sort of got to the stage where they had to get the stuff in, so they had to pay up. These blokes know that.

On the frontier, like on the border from Ecuador into Colombia, the Custom officers and that, they used to hang out for money. I mean, make the company sweat, because they knew the company wanted to get their machinery to work, so they'd hold out for the best price. Anyway, the company agreed to pay whatever it was they were asking, so we got into Colombia.

We were there three weeks trying to get through. We have to drive all the rigs through into Colombia, and all the trucks were there waiting. They wouldn't come into Ecuador to load. We had to take our stuff into Colombia to load. So we were loading there for about two days, and when we took off there was a convoy of trucks and cars, because all of us had to be transported as well. Some of the drivers still came from Ecuador, but they were only on the road a day, and then they had to go back because we were getting, like employing people as we went.

But you couldn't travel on a Sunday. They wouldn't let you travel on a Sunday and all the cops were … sort of corrupt. I mean, I can remember one time there when we were driving from Guayaquil to Chone, I drove my ute, because we could only take it as it was pretty limited on the barge, you know when they'd send the barge out to the island to pick the vehicle up. So we could put only one ute on, and I had the two power plants in a buggy; that was one load for the barge.

I had a driver, Rodriquez his name was, and he drove the buggy, because those buggies are very limited to their speed. They could only do probably 40 mile an hour and it was a pretty slow trip from Guayaquil to Chone.

The buggies, they transport all the heavy stuff. Like they've got tanks on them. For the drilling you had to have water, so they had tanks on it, but they could also pull trailers and things like that.

The buggies were a special four-wheel-drive truck. They were a funny-looking thing. They looked like a tractor – big tractor tyres on them – but you could go anywhere with them, you know. They were really powerful little motors.

Yeah, Rodriquez drove the buggy with the lighting plant, or the power plant, on it from the camp, because it had two big CAT motors, see, and while one was being serviced the other one would kick in. That was for the freezers and for the cook and for lights and all that sort of stuff. Anyway, we came to this check gate there, and this bloke wanted to see my licence, so I pulled out my New South Wales licence. This was before the photo licence.

It was just like a piece of paper, because he couldn't read English, so he's turning this thing upside down and sideways and he couldn't understand it, and I said, 'Well, that's my licence.' I just played dumb. I could understand him, but I wasn't letting on, so I'd just sort of say, 'Well, that's my licence,' and I was talking English and he couldn't understand me, but I could understand what he was talking about, and I knew what he wanted.

So Rodriquez came up and Rodriquez knew what he wanted, so he just gave him a couple of bucks. Well, probably, I think, a couple of hundred sucres, and of course he was quite happy with that, because they're so corrupt over there. I mean, you could buy your way out of just about anything.

Anyway, getting back to the loading at the Colombian border. We loaded up and took off from there, and we were going through Colombia and, of course, we weren't allowed to travel on a Sunday. That was a rest day. It took us a week to go right through by truck to a place called Caqueta, and that was on the Colombian/Venezuela border. So we went right through Colombia by truck, which was a great experience. It took us a week.

Some of it was very mountainous. Some of it wasn't bad. I was expecting the road to be terrible, but no, they weren't too bad at all.

There was a lot of it jungle and a lot of the country was farmland. Most of it was market gardens, like, and of course they grow everything there themselves, like bananas, pineapple, that sort of stuff. But no, there's a lot of ranches but it's nothing to see people, I mean, walking along the road there. All the time you see them. There was one place in particular we went through, it was just a village on a big river, and they were all like African, you know, the grass huts they make in Africa? They were all black, all fullblood and I suppose they went back to the slave trade.

They looked like Negroes. They were all in this one area. They are great market gardeners, because of the water. They had no shortage of water and, just looking at the design of the huts, it was just like a village in Africa. Yeah, and they were all real black, kinky hair and everything. Anyway, it would be nothing to see them fellas walking along the road with a big basket on their heads, especially the women, full of vegetables, taking them to market. Like, both sides of the camp, they'd transport all their stuff in on foot. Some of them had money. Some had a donkey, you know. An old donkey would carry their stuff in, yeah.

Anyway we had what they call aduana [Customs] guards. I've got photos of them, actually. Aduana guards are all in uniform, like government, like a Customs officer, but not Customs. They were to make sure that we didn't do anything [wrong] going through Colombia, like, stopping to do a job or, like selling stuff through their country. Well, there was four of these with the crew and I was travelling in, what do they call those little cars? They're the cheapest car you can buy in South America, anyway. A Renault. Yes, one of those. Anyway it was a funny little car. There was me and two aduana guards and the mechanic in it. The mechanic was a Colombian. Chiparro, we called him. There was another car with two others and, I think Zane, the party manager, was in one and somebody else was in the other. But anyway, there was two vehicles travelling with us, and all the big towns we went through there, it was a fantastic trip. I had to come back there; I came back to Colombia and I worked there for a while.

I had to come back there from Venezuela for they were having trouble in a couple of camps and I had to come back to help them out. You see, I was going to Venezuela as … I wasn't drilling. There was no rigs there, it was all vibrasies, and they're like big shakers; they are like big praying mantis; there was four of them. They go along and everything is computerised. They drive along about ten foot and they'd all stop and they'd all jack up together. They had a big steel plate underneath and that plate used to hit the ground and jack up, and all the vehicles would all go up together. Everything was timed perfect because of the computerised system they had in it; all electronics. It was unreal.

They'd go along and all the drivers had to do was steer them. Like, just put them into gear and just drive along and they'd stop themselves, jack up, and they'd shake for about probably five or ten seconds and then they'd go down and the plate would come up and they'd go along another ten foot and they'd stop and they'd all go up together again. It was unreal.

Anyway, I was working with them and I was there as a trainee technician. It was a big change from the drilling rigs. I was working with a technician, a bloke called Mike Netterville. He was an American bloke, but a really great guy. He worked in South America, I think, when he started. He was with Western ever since he was about fifteen, sixteen, or something. But he was only a young bloke; he was only in his early twenties. But him and I we mated up together because I was working with him, and we'd just walk along or drive along. Most times we'd walk alongside of the machinery, just, you know, follow them along. Then one would drop out and a mechanic would service that and then he'd go back into line and then the other one would drop out. It was like that; it was non-stop.

When production started I was looking after the cable crew, which they call the jug line. There was about 100 blokes on the jug line, and they used to go along and put the cables in the ground and hook it all up to the recorder. Well, when these things would shake they'd get all the things that travel through the cables into the recorder and it came out on graph paper, like all the little lines and that, and it told you if there was a show there, like if there was any oil underneath. If it was worth drilling they'd bring a big rig in there to drill the oil well.

I was doing that for quite a while. Once, I was wondering why ... even the observer and the shooter said, 'There's something wrong because we've fallen too far behind.' Usually the cable crew were sort of a couple of mile in front of you, because once you started shaking, like, a recording, you just kept going. These blokes were sent ahead and they were always a couple of mile ahead of you so you didn't have any hold-ups and we were catching them up all the time. So anyway, I went up to find out what the trouble was and I caught a bloke shooting up. He was a heroin addict.

He was Ecuadorian [or a] Venezuelan bloke. Anyway, they were on the heavy stuff, you know. They weren't smoking just dope they were shooting up. Anyway, I end up firing 90 blokes off the line; I sacked them. I used to take a truckload in and bring a truckload back because you'd just have to walk along the street over there, I mean, there's so many people out of work. Like, a couple of hundred bucks a month, that was big money for them. Anyway, we had no trouble picking blokes up, but the hardest part was teaching them what to do.

So anyway, a couple of other boys came in – even the party manager came in and it didn't take long to show them what to do. It was only walking along, running along cables and pushing them into the ground. When the shooter would go along the other half of the crew would come along and roll the cables up and go ahead and lay them out again. You know, it was like that: pick up and drop off, pick up and drop off. It didn't take long. Anyway, the production went from corner to corner on the chart and I was a white-headed boy. I got a pat on the head from Houston. They gave me a gold watch because of the production. The production just jumped straight to the top after we got rid of the druggos.

I had the watch stolen; it was snapped off my arm. I went to sleep on the bonnet of the ute one night and it got ripped off. I had a few beers and I was tired and I [was] just sort of laying back on the bonnet of the ute waiting for the other boys to come out of this beer joint and one of the fellas saw the watch and I suppose he liked it, so he took it. I chased him but there was no way of catching him. Anyway, I lost the watch. That's another story.

Well, because I didn't like what I was doing there, because I liked the drill rigs, and because I wanted to go to Rio, but I couldn't go to Rio because they had a full crew there, I asked Dieter if I could go and he said, 'No, you can't.' So he said, 'Colombia or Venezuela.' So I was in Venezuela, but used to come back into Colombia. When you go to Venezuela you've got to have a medical to get into the country, like, to work in the country. All your visas and that are fixed up for you.

Maracaibo and Cartagena

They send you back – there's one plane from this place, from Maracaibo, to this joint over on the Caribbean coast of Colombia. They had a doctor there. There was only one plane, and it went in on a Friday and dropped you off, and then it came back the next Friday. I had to go there for a week and it wasn't very hard to take because the Caribbean coast of Colombia was just beautiful you know. Being on the coast in a nice big flash hotel and everything was paid for you.

If you were a foreigner, you had to have a medical to work in Venezuela. You couldn't get your medical in Venezuela; you had to go out of the country. So they had it teed up; the company had it teed up with this doctor in Cartagena.

In Maracaibo I went into the office because I had to go and get this medical. So the accountant said, 'How much money do you reckon you'll need for the week?' I thought, well, gee, they were paying for everything and I said, 'Well, I don't know. I don't even know the place.' He said, 'Well, we pay everything,' he said, 'we pay for your meals, your accommodation, your fare over and back. We give you a return ticket, but you've got to stay there for the week because there's only one plane a week.'

So, anyway, he said, 'I'll give you a couple of grand and see how you go with that.' Of course you've got to account for everything. You've got to bring the receipts back and if you've got any change, well, you've got to give it back. I mean, they don't give it to you to keep. But that was a fantastic place.

So I went there and this [doctor] bloke was getting paid by the company, so he was a bit of a sly old fox and it was no trouble getting your medical. I mean, you go in there and he'd just examine you and he'd say, 'Well, you're all right,' and just write you out a medical and then you were gone and you just sat around and drank beer and chased women at the pool. You had the beach there, and all the hotels were right on the beach, but they had the big pools in the hotels. They were fantastic places. I mean, you got waited on hand and foot and the meals … the food was fantastic.

The whole city had a big high brick wall or stone wall around it because the Spaniards were there. They had even old cannons all around the wall. You know, it was like a big fort, the old part of the city, and real little narrow streets. But as time went by they started building outside of the walls. The old part of the city was Cartagena itself. It was called after an Indian princess, as a matter of fact. They've got a big statue of her in the middle of the city.

It was a fantastic place. But for a week, I mean, it wasn't very hard to take, I can tell you. When you went on break, like, in those countries there, your month is 21 days. They count your month as 21 days, not 28 days. It's a bit strange, but this is the working system they had. So we used to work … in some countries there we worked two weeks on and one week off and other places we worked three weeks and one week off. It was all depends what country you were in. In Venezuela, it was two on and one off; in Colombia it was three on and one off; in Ecuador, it was three on and one off.

Then they'd pay you … your airfare was paid back to your base back to your main office, which in Ecuador it was Quito. We worked out of Quito, like, all over the place. In Colombia it was Bogota, and we worked all over the place. In Venezuela it was Maracaibo, and we worked all over the place. Well what we used to do, Mike and I, because of Caqueta – and we liked Caqueta and we knew a couple of girls there – we used to get paid and take our money in the airfare, like, instead of getting our ticket we used to take the money. Because you'd fly from a place called Calabozo and we used to fly back to Caracas and then from Caracas to Maracaibo.

Well, we'd take our airfare to Caracas and then we'd take the other half in cash. We'd go to Caracas and then catch another plane then to San Antonio, which was on the frontier border of Colombia and Venezuela. Of course, we'd jump [the border], it being frontier. Landing in San Antonio, in Venezuela, you didn't have to have a visa to jump back over into Colombia. You'd go both sides of the border there. Like, you'd go over to San Antonio and you'd see Colombian cars driving around; you'd go over to Caqueta and you'd see all the Venezuelan cars driving around. So you had no trouble getting backwards and forwards.

We used to get paid $1000 our month, which was 21 days. Well, when we went on our break they'd pay us our living allowance, which was $1000. That was on top of our wages. You didn't have to touch your wages. All your wages were sent back … because we used to get paid from Houston in US dollars and that went straight to whatever bank you wanted. In my case – I was living in Dubbo in New South Wales – so my money went back to the bank in Dubbo, to my bank, and I lived on my living allowance, which was quite healthy, because in those countries it was so cheap.

It all depends what country you were in. Like, if it was expensive, like Venezuela was well, it [the living allowance] went up and down. If you were in Ecuador it wasn't so much. I think we were only getting about $700 US a month there, because it was cheap. Venezuela was a more expensive country, so it went up to $1000. Like, a bottle of beer over there was only 30 cents. A packet of cigarettes was only about 28 cents. A gallon of petrol was only about 3 cents.

Caqueta and Casual 'Wives'

Mike and I, like, when we'd do this we used to jump off at Caracas and fly back to San Antonio and then jump the border back into Caqueta, and we used to say our wives would be joining us later, because they were flying from Ecuador. We used to call these girls our wives because when we'd book into the hotel it was pretty hard to get girls in there, so we used to say that they were flying in and that our wives would be joining us later.

We'd book a double room, you see, so we were sort of one jump ahead of them and they were none the wiser. When the women would come, like, the girls, I mean, we knew them from before, months before when we were coming through there, and they lived in Caqueta. We were in Caqueta and they were just out in the cathouse. Nice girls they were; very beautiful women. Mike and I sort of stuck to the ones we knew before. That's how we used to get them into the hotel.

We'd pay for the hotel room as a married couple and these girls … we'd just go out and pick them up because we used to hire a Volkswagen in San Antonio and drive it over the border. That was our transport around. Anyway, that was how. We told the girls, 'Pack a bag', and they'd walk in like they'd just come off the plane, see, and then we lived there for the week with them, or they lived with us. It was good. So you had to be sort of one step ahead of them otherwise they wouldn't let the women in.

Yes, they were very strict about that sort of thing, because they were really nice places. I mean, big flash hotels and a lot of tourists, so they didn't want blokes coming in with women from those sort of joy houses. Yeah, it was all right though. I mean, nobody got into trouble and we just took the girls back and next break we'd come and do the same thing again, so we always had the same women, so they were none the wiser, which was great.

Once Mike and I, instead of flying back to Caracas to join our crew we decided to take the Volkswagen to Maracaibo and, I think, it cost us $1.50 for fuel to go from San Antonio to Maracaibo. Maracaibo was our base and I had about 40 days break up my sleeve. But before that I was going to Libya to join the drilling crews again. The company called me on the two-way and said that there was a position for me in Libya and did I object to going there? I said, 'No,' you know, I'd go. So I was all sort of set to go and then they called back the day after and said, 'Well, you can't go there now because there's a war on.' So they wouldn't let you into those sort of dangerous areas.

So, anyway, I had 40 days break, so I went back to [inaudible] Mike and I, we drove to Maracaibo. He was getting shifted. I think he had to go back to Houston and I was going to go with him actually, but I wanted to come home to see my kids. We were going to drive to the Grand Ole Opry in Nashville. He had his ute at home and I was breaking my neck to get to the Grand Ole Opry, like, the Country Music Hall of Fame, and see all the greatest there, all the photos and that. I was looking forward to doing that. That was our idea. I was going to go, but I was homesick and I wanted to come home, so the company paid my fare home. I thought I was going back to South America but when I got home my break was just about up.

When I came home in '82 – when I left Venezuela – like I said, Mike and I hired this Volkswagen and we drove to Maracaibo and that was the last time I saw him, because then I came home. I was on leave and I had 40 days accumulated leave and so they paid my fare home. I was going to take the airfare and go to Nashville but I didn't; I decided to come home. So I came home and just before my time was up to go back they sent – I've still got the ticket actually – the return ticket, and I kept it. I don't know, they probably got their money back, I don't know, but I've still got the ticket made out back to Houston, actually. In that time there, too, I spent a couple of months in Houston because of the drilling rigs, the Adcos, we were getting – like, go there with a mechanic. We had a couple of months there just to go through and find out how everything worked and that. That was a good experience, too.

It was seventeen months I had in South America all together. It was seventeen months over two visits.

Home and Family

When I came home and my time was just about up and I was ready to go back to South America, back to my crew, I got a telegram from Houston saying to go to such and such a travel agency in Dubbo and pick up a ticket and fly to Perth. So I flew to Perth and I went to the office, because Western had an office in Perth, you see, and I had to go over there. So, I went to Perth and walked in the office there and they gave me a ticket to Singapore. So, I didn't know where the bloody hell I was going to finish up.

When I got back from there, like, from South America before I went to Singapore, it was good to catch up with the kids because I hadn't seen them for eleven months. It was almost twelve months, and I was surprised to see how much they'd grown and I think they were just as excited as I was because Dad was coming home. At that stage, like, I used to stay with the kids at home, like, in Val's house, but not living as man and wife. We were just keeping friends for the kids' sake. Anyway, there was six kids: her two, I reared them up, Gina and David. David was only about eighteen months old, I think, when Val and I got together. I used to treat them as my own kids.

Gina and David were the two eldest ones and the other kids were Tracey, she was the oldest girl; then Casey, he was the oldest boy; and Valecia and Justin and Megan and Clayton. Actually, Megan and Clayton, they're Western Australians. They were both born in Western Australia, up in Paraburdoo where I worked before. They were scattered, actually, because there was two born in Quirindi, one in Townsville, two in Western Australia and two in Dubbo.

So they were sort of scattered; and one in Werris Creek. So they were sort of scattered around.

Everybody used to say, 'Well, when all these kids grow up they're going to have itchy feet because they travelled so much when they were small.' They were back and forwards over the Nullarbor and up into Paraburdoo and Perth. Now, they all live up in Coffs Harbour. The girls got married and had kids. My three grandsons: Johnny and Shane and Stewart. I just hope sometime later on in life that they're going to come across this interview. It would be great for them to hear what their grandad done: working everywhere and chasing women all over the world!

I came to Sydney, and because I came out of Venezuela … Remember before, I was telling you about the injections that I had to have, well, when you came out of those places they kept an eye on you in case you had that disease and they didn't want you to spread it around Australia. So when I came to Sydney and I was coming through Customs, and they knew I came out of Venezuela, I showed them my medical card, you know, the injections that I had, but that didn't make any difference, you still had to go into quarantine for a week.

So they gave me the option to either go down to Melbourne or go to Canberra. Because of Chris and his family being in Canberra I decided to go to Canberra and stay the week with them. That was because of all the trouble they were having over there in Venezuela there with the cholera, typhoid and yellow fever and all that sort of stuff, see. The reason being, that they didn't want you to go to, like, up the coast somewhere, the high [north] country, you had to come to the low [south] country because of the mosquitoes or something. Cooler country, and less chance of infecting mosquitoes. They [the mosquitoes] sort of transport the disease around. That was the reason why I had to go to either Melbourne or Canberra, but everything was paid for. The Customs there, they gave me a return ticket from Sydney to Canberra, and have the week there. I had to pay my own accommodation, but I only had the one night in the motel and then I moved in with Chris and his family. I lost my watch there, yeah [in the motel].

Singapore and Indonesia

So I got to Singapore and I walked in the office there on Scotts Road in Singapore and they give me another ticket to Indonesia. So I finished up in Indonesia for twelve months; Indonesia. Like, based in Singapore but working in Indonesia. They used to always fly me back to Singapore because it was my base. There our wages were the same, but our living allowance altered. It wasn't very much – it was only about $500 in Singapore – living allowance. I thought it should have been $1000 because the accommodation was more expensive there, and everything else.

The little place we were staying at in Indonesia, called Runtapunya – it was Asamera Oil [Asamera Oil (Indonesia) Ltd] – and that's the people we were in there working for. They were the clients that Western was working for and it's a very, very rich oil field in that part of Indonesia. And in the morning the helicopter, a big Asamera helicopter, used to take the people in to Madang so they could catch another plane to Singapore, like when we'd go on our break. And early in the morning, about 4 o'clock, the helicopter'd take off and a lot of the times, if we could get a seat on it, we used to go by helicopter back to Madang, just get a ride instead of going by car. And early in the morning you'd go – you know you'd take off from Runtapunya and go up and you'd see all the oilfield, like the whole lot of the oilfield. You'd see the gas burning on the wells. It was just unreal to see how many wells that were there.

The wells were all on land but, there was one shot there that I did … I drove past this line that was already shot and one of the holes, 60 foot hole that was,

With water buffalo, Indonesia, middle of the oil fields, Sumatra, 1983.

Billy with work crew in Indonesia, 1983.

and crude [oil] was coming out of it. Yeah, it was just so shallow. The amount of oil there in that place is just unreal. Yeah, so we used to go back to Singapore, but a lot of the times – like if your six months was up the company'd fly you home, but I think I only came once, no, twice. Once I paid my own fare home, which was only about $600 then, like return from Singapore to Sydney. I'd accumulated a bit of leave and I decided to fly home, so I paid my own fare. But, yeah, we were so close then, see. I mean it was a lot easier because you were only sort of seven hours from home, which was great.

That was in '82. The reason why I flew home was because it was Christmas. That was when I paid my own fare home. I accumulated the leave there so I could get home for Christmas, but it wasn't six months. If it was six months the company'd pay, you see. So anyway I did, that was the reason why I paid my own fare. I went home for Christmas and then I flew back and unknownst [sic] to me that the contract was … Well, we had other contracts to do but they cancelled them.

So then when I flew back I done January, February, March and then I came home on 28 March. That's when I came home and stayed. Anyway, I'd sort of had enough of it, my almost three years living away in different countries and that, and I'd seen a lot of it so, yeah, I wasn't really worried. We were supposed to go – like the Australians were supposed to go – to Delhi in India, but they wouldn't let the Australians in there to work. They wouldn't give us visas.

They reckoned that there was too many of their own people out of work. The company had been in there before and they had trained local people. See, most of the time we were just sort of like supervising the people to teach them. You trained a lot of people and you'd make drillers out of them. Well then, they were sort of doing us out of a job really. But that was the way the company worked because they could get them to work for them a lot cheaper than we would, see, but we were silly. We should never have done it. We were doing ourselves out of a job.

I had to sign a contract, a two-year contract, even though they didn't hold you to it, but they used to prefer you to go for a least two years because then they say that you'd save them a large amount of money in the local labour.

Yeah, when we was working in Runtapunya we had local pilots, Indonesian pilots, and they were pretty rough sort of pilots. They were, you know. They're only little blokes, about five foot nothing, but very cocky people. If they was a pilot or a doctor, or you know, something pretty high up, they thought they was just the ant's pants. But anyway, this one pilot I had there in Indonesia, we run into a mob of fruit bats once, but luckily nothing happened. I didn't come down or anything.

All the helipads in the jungle were made out of the timber, big thick logs. They were cut and made into like a flat top, so the chopper could come down and land and drop supplies like fuel and stuff like that, and food, and whatever you wanted for the crews. And my ice used to come out sort of every second day. I used to get an esky full of ice and butter and stuff like that, because it wouldn't keep very long. I think about twelve days was the longest I stayed out in a fly camp in Indonesia. Then they made me come in. They said, 'Well, you've had enough. You've got to come in.' So it was, well, you done what you were told, but we were having a lot of trouble [drilling holes] in one place there and I stayed out probably longer than I should have done. But anyway, the company said, 'Well, you've got to come in.' So, anyway, they sent the chopper out and I came in.

But this bloke, this one pilot, when he took off from the helipad, he tipped the chopper to one side and the blade hit the leaves on the tree and sort of … the helicopter sort of swayed around a bit and I tell you what, I was packing 'em because I thought we were gone. Anyway, he got it out. He got it up and when we got home I said to the party manager, 'Well, in future,' I said, 'I don't want that pilot.' And he said, 'Why?' and I told him. I said, 'Well, once,' I said, 'he run into,' – I mean it wasn't his fault really – 'the bats.' you know, he should have took more care, I thought. But then with the tree I thought, 'Well, that's the last straw, because this bloke'll end up killing me.' I told the party manager and he said, 'Right, if he's that bad,' he said, 'we'll get rid of him.' So he got the sack, and I was quite pleased to see him go actually, because [he was] not like the pilot I had over in South America.

I had a bloke in South America that flew rescue choppers in the Alps. He was a Frenchman and he was a really good pilot. The only fault that bloke had, he used to love garlic, and in the chopper – I mean you had your earphones on

– but, I mean it'd nearly knock you over, the smell, you know, putting up with the smell. He used to eat garlic, pieces of garlic, like apple. He loved the stuff. But you couldn't fault him. He was a great pilot. A lot of the times there, like, he saved me many miles. Mostly he used to drop in at a helipad, but where it was clear enough and where he could get down sort of a foot above the ground, he'd just bring the chopper down and sit there and I'd just jump out and then he'd go. 'Same place this afternoon,' and he'd come back to the same spot and do the same thing and pick me up. So he sort of, he more or less dropped me right with the crews, instead of having to walk a long way.

Yeah, he was a great old bloke. I even used to go when he'd test his chopper. I can remember one day there in the camp in Chone, the mechanics were working on the chopper so he had to take it for a test flight. So, he said, 'Come on Billy,' he said, 'come with me and we'll go and test the chopper.' So I jumped in with him and he went straight up for about almost 1000 feet, straight up in the air. He never went sideways, he just went straight up, and I'm sitting down, I'm watching the ground sort of disappear from underneath me. And it was just unreal, straight up in the air, yeah. But he was a great pilot. He knew his job. He used to fly people in rescue, like skiers and that, like who'd have a smash. He used to fly choppers there.

Dubious Dealings

Getting back to Indonesia, could you imagine a blackfella in Singapore when I was setting up the crew to go into Runtapunya in Indonesia? We were getting all new, well I thought new rigs and that, like new little – what do they call them? – Briggs & Stratton motors, like for the pumps and to drive the rig itself. And it was my job to make sure we had everything, like all the right tools and the right equipment and that for the crew. So I had to stay back with the party manager and supervise all the machineries.

When we got all the stuff to Runtapunya it came in on the barge and I was unloading this stuff. It all came in crates. And then I could see like inspection plates missing off the pumps and, you know, like they were all second-hand stuff just repainted. And I'd thought it was all new stuff that we were getting. All new stuff because like with new stuff you'd be saying, 'Well, you know, we got a good run here because there won't be any breakdowns.' See, if you had new machines and that you could work sort of with no hold ups, which was good for us because it made us better, because we could get more production. Anyway, I said to the party manager, I said, 'What's going on here?' I said, 'I thought all this stuff was new,' because we'd just walk into a place and say, 'Well, look, we want, you know, twenty pumps and twenty motors.'

And well, anyway, we got all this second-hand stuff and I think – I wouldn't like to say for sure – but I think that's why the area manager there in Singapore got the sack, because he was doing a deal. This is how shifty he was and he was a very wealthy man. I mean, he had a travel agency there in Singapore, this bloke; he had an exploration boat that he leased to Western and he had export Colombian coffee and all that sort of stuff, and he had a shop with this other Chinese bloke. One bloke was American and the other fellow was Chinese and I think they done a swiftie on the company. I think they bought all this stuff and they just went over them and reconditioned them and then spray painted them and sent them out to us in Indonesia. I think that's how they done it and I think he got found out and that's why he got the sack, because it wasn't long after that he did get the sack.

They made this new rig they called the AS 10 and they sold these to the company as well, 'cause we had about twenty of them in Indonesia. But the Briggs and Stratton motors weren't any good to drive, because they were all old and reconditioned and that.

So anyway, I decided to try the new Hondas, so I went to Madang and I bought four Honda motors; 10 horsepower Hondas, like one for the rig and one for the pump for each crew. I put these and two crews in different areas and when the production jumped up, well, the company said, 'Well, that's the way to go.' So they turned around and bought 20 more. So we ended up with new Hondas, 10 horsepower Hondas, which was really great.

This bloke, this guy that got the sack, he was like asking me about the rig and how it worked and everything and I said that it could go to 200 feet in a six and three-quarter-inch hole. I said, 'It'd be the type of thing you'd want in Melbourne. You'd want it down in Melbourne to drill water bores.' I knew that they were having trouble [getting] water, and they would have been ideal over in Australia. Yeah, these little AS 10s they had, they designed them and a little rotary rig. I asked him, this bloke – I won't mention his name – but this American guy, the bloke that designed them, he got the sack from Western and I was going to bring a couple of those little rigs over and work them in Melbourne for him. I could run the show over here, see, because I think I could have made some money with those little rigs, like for backyard water, 'cause they would have been ideal, but they don't make them anymore. The company'd still have them. They were great little machines.

Anyway, he asked me to test one. When I told him it could go to 200 foot with a six and three-quarter-inch bit, he wanted to see it. So anyway, the Chinese bloke that he was in shares with … they had a finger in the pie all over the place, because they were pretty shrewd operators. He had a big aviary there, this bloke, and he had birds from everywhere, like all over Asia, this Chinese guy, so that's where I took the rig to test it. So I had to dig a couple of pits and I tested it. I went to 200 foot and they were quite happy with it. They paid me $500 for the few days and paid my accommodation to set the rig up and everything. So, yeah, I wasn't complaining. That was on my way home, see, so it just sort of fell in nicely. They asked me how much I wanted and I said, 'Well, how much do you reckon?' and they said, 'Well, will $500 be enough?' and I said, 'Yeah, that'll be fine', and accommodation of course, and keep. Yeah, that was good.

PART THREE

For the drought is on the station and the weather's growing hotter,
But we're bound to get the water deeper down.

– Banjo Paterson

Home to Stay – Business Venture

When we couldn't get into Delhi, like a lot of the boys there … The company tried to get us in there but the Indian government wouldn't let us in; wouldn't give us work visas to go in there. So they said, 'Well look, you know, go home, take your break and if something comes up we'll call you.' So I'd sort of had enough and I thought, 'Well, I'm not really interested in going back. I've seen it all, I've done it all.' So I decided to buy my own drill rig and work for myself, like run the thing myself. So I had a bit of money and I had to borrow a bit more, so me and another guy … I went back and I worked for Watermins for a while when I came back, which was a company in Orange, a water drilling company [Watermin Drillers Pty Ltd]. I worked for them for a while and I applied for this loan and I tried to get it through the Aboriginal Land Council I was dealing with in Dubbo. I applied for it. Actually, before that I tried to buy a property, because I had a few quid when I came back and I tried to buy this property and Uncle 'Ope was helping me and he said, 'The best thing you can do,' he said, 'is go to Canberra and sit on their doorstep and pester them.' He said, 'You'll get the money.'

But, anyway, I wasn't prepared to do that, so all I done was went to the office in Dubbo and I asked them. I checked it out and they said, 'Well look, you're halfway there,' and the white blokes that were working for the organisation there in Dubbo, they thought that I had a good chance. So I applied for the money and I wanted to borrow $120,000, which is a lot of money. But the place

I was after was out in between Bourke and Weilmoringle and it was on the Culgoa River. Only small, but it would have been a good property. I had enough money, my own money, to stock the place, but I wanted enough money to buy the place. Anyway, they wrote me a letter back and said that they could lend me $75,000, but I had to wait until the funds were available. So then I went off that because I knew it was a lot of money.

I did try for a dry-cleaning shop in Gilgandra. There was a dry-cleaning shop for sale and it had a two-bedroom house and the front of it was a dry cleaner's place. So yeah, I was going to have a go at that, too. I was going to buy that there, but that fell through. Then I decided on the drilling rig because it was my trade and I knew it well and I decided to go for the rig instead. So I went for something that I knew something about.

My brother-in-law in Dubbo, Val's brother Kenny Grant, well he was working for Watermins, too, yeah, and I told him about this rig that I wanted. He saw the rig in the paper and he told me about it, so we jumped in the car and went up to Quirindi, up near Tamworth. That's where the rig was for sale. As soon as I saw the rig and I tested it out … I put a little [drill hole] down there in the backyard and it was ideal because it was only a 500, which is a small rig. It could go to 500 feet, and that suited us, or suited me to the ground, because most water bores around are, you know, 300 and 400 feet, so you still had 100 up your sleeve. No water bores around that I knew of was 500 feet. Like out west, yes, but not around these areas. Anyway, I bought the rig with this bloke in shares.

Stan Murray was his name. He come from Melbourne originally, but I met him in Albury/Wodonga, down on the border. When I told him about it I said I was waiting to have the money come through and he said, 'Well, if you're looking for a partner,' he said, 'I'm interested.' So I thought, well his wife used to work for the Clyde Cameron College. She was an accountant and she was a very smart cookie, actually. Anyway, I decided to take this guy on because it would make it easier for me to borrow the money, because I didn't have to borrow so much, see. He borrowed his share and I borrowed mine, and that's how we kicked off.

We ended up buying the rig and he came up to Quirindi. Him and his father came up. They drove up and then he drove the rig back to Wodonga in Victoria and that's where we kicked off in 1984. We kicked off, in winter, in June '84, 1984.

You know, we battled because of our payments, our repayments. We had to get out and sell the work. We were prepared to cut the prices a little bit to get the work, so we ... yeah, we done alright, I mean, for a new company starting off. I named the company. Being the founder of the company, I named it Dakota Drillers. Just kicking off, like a new company and no one knew us, we had to get out and sell the work. We went out and booked into country pubs, like all the cockies'd come in on the weekend and we sort of mingled with them and got to know them. We just offered our services to them and a lot of them took us on.

This was all down around Wodonga, like around Chiltern, Corowa, Beechworth, all over, mostly in Victoria, and then we came up to Gundagai 'cause they were carting water there at a little place just out of Gundagai. It's right on the highway just out of Gundagai. I forget the name of it. Anyway, we're nine miles from Gundagai. Know the Tuckerbox there? Yeah, well, where the dog sits on the tuckerbox? Well, we even done one for the people there that were running the ... They bought a railway carriage and they made it into a restaurant and they had a little shop and they wanted water, too. So we done a water bore for them, there in Gundagai. But, anyway, this little place I was telling you about, they were carting water by truck to their houses, and one bloke took us on, then the people next door. We done three jobs, just jumped through the fence, and we done three in a line.

We ended up doing seven bores there in this little town. I just can't think of the name of it. It'll come to me later. Anyway, we done that and we were back and forwards in New South Wales and Victoria, 'cause I was licensed in New South Wales to drill. You had to have a driller's licence. So then I applied for my licence down there and I got that no problem, so I was licensed in two states, which helped us a lot. Yeah, and then – yeah, the name of that little place, I just thought of it – it was Coolac. We done seven bores there in Coolac and one at the roadhouse there, or the restaurant, the little – what do they call that, Snake Gully? And we done one for Leightons, the contractors with all the earthmoving gear. They built all the roads.

Yeah, well, they were doing the road there, working on the highway, and they run out of water. There was a lot of bushfires around there, too, at the time. And these fellas [Leightons] wanted water, so we got a good job off them. Like we put our price up and we got what we asked and we done a job for them, which was really good, yeah, because they had to have water for the roads, see, to keep the dust down.

   Then we went up to Dubbo because I knew a lot of cockies around Dubbo, especially out around Eumungerie and Mogriguy and those places. We done quite a few jobs up there. The first year we turned over $90,000 and the second year we got up to $105,000, so it wasn't too bad for a couple of new fellas in the game. My partner's wife, she was very strict with the cash. She didn't like to … I mean, when you made the money she was quite happy, but when you wanted to spend some of it to look after machinery she didn't like parting with it. So she and I had a bit of a fall out, because my idea was to maintain the rig properly, like if it broke down then you'd be sitting around waiting for parts.

   If you knew something was, you know, like wearing out, well, you sent away and you replaced it so you wouldn't break down, but she just didn't want to spend the money. Like, you had to have spare bits on the rig because you had to get your bits from either Melbourne or Sydney, from big companies that make those sort of things. You couldn't buy them in Albury/Wodonga 'cause a bit'd cost you $800, like for a big bit, like tungsten tip tricones or tungsten tip drag bits, and you had to have a spare one on the rig so if one bit was wearing out, before it wore out completely you sent away and you got another one. Sitting, waiting for it to come, you know, and that was a hold up. But that's the sort of person she was. Anyway, I had a fall out with her and I took off. They still owe me a lot of money but I don't think I'll ever get it, but, anyway, that's part of life, I suppose.

Back to Bourke

Yeah, after working there for a few years with the drilling rig I took off. I was going back to Bourke to trap birds because there was big money in it, but you had to be licensed and I didn't know that.

So I pulled out of the rig to go back to do that and then when I found out you had to have a licence it sort of didn't interest me much any more. I'm in Bourke for two days and my nephew Barry Gray was leaving the company he was working for there. With the cottonseed they used to make diesel and they used to make fertiliser out of the stuff; they got the oil out to make the diesel. Yeah, so anyway, he said, 'Look, you want a job?' and he said, 'I'm pulling out.' He said, 'I'm going back shearing.' And I said, 'Yeah, well, I'll go and have a look at it.' So I went and Barry introduced me to the bloke that was running the show there and said, like, 'This is my uncle from so and so.' Anyway the bloke said, 'Well, yeah', he said, 'you got the job if you want it.' So I started the next day. Ended up staying there for a while.

I worked there and it sort of slackened off a bit because it was the end of the cotton season. Then he gave me a job pulling the old gaol house down; cleaning the bricks at the old gaol house in Bourke, down where I went to school actually, not far from the convent school. I was there pulling old bars out of the windows and cleaning the bricks, pushing the walls over and that, and just cleaning the bricks and stacking them. I did that for about a month I suppose.

And then I left that and went to work for Westbeef [pastoral company] on the cotton, because the season was starting up again. See, one season finished and you'd go back and start again next season. So then they had to gas all the ground,[41] and you know, like stick-picking and that and clearing other parts there for the next season. So I got a job there and I was with them for about twelve months. Yeah, it was good going there.

I lived with my sister there, yeah, with Joanie. She was living back in Tudor Street right next door to the old place where we was reared up. Yeah, she lived in a Commission house there run by the Widjeri [Co-op], by the Aboriginal people, and she was leasing that off them. So, yeah, I went back and I moved in with Joanie and her son Checker and his wife Corny.

I stayed with them for a while and there was a whole house out at a place called Longmeadow out towards the weir, and the company owned that. Westbeef owned it and there was no one living there so I asked the boss. I went and I asked him if I could rent it out. The old boss was old George Rice. I went to school with him, so I had no trouble getting the place and they only charged me $30 a week. It was just for paying for the power. I bought a bit of second-hand furniture around town, like a bed and mattress and a dressing table. I got a lend of a fridge off my cousin, off Yvonne, Yvonne Knight, and I got a lend of tables and chairs off Checker and Corny. So, yeah, it ended up quite good. I had my own place there and I stayed there for a while and then had to leave, so I left and went back down to Orange.

---

41. 'Gas the ground' – a term used when preparing land for cotton growing.

Kalgoorlie – Orange – Heart Attack

I was running out of money. I had a white station wagon at the time, an XD Falcon, and I back-traded it to get a bit of cash in my pocket. And blow me down, after I back-traded the car, two days later I got a job in Kalgoorlie. I'd walked into a wreckers in Orange there and I didn't know that an old mate of mine owned it; used to work for Watermins. The two of them, the mechanic and one of the drillers, they'd bought the place and I didn't know this. So I walked in there and Maurie Morell, he was in there – Maurie Maher his name was, but we called him Maurie Morell – and Mick O'Shannessy, they owned the place.

So Maurie said to me, he said, 'You wouldn't be looking for a job?' and I said, 'Well, as a matter of fact, I am,' and he said, 'Well, go and get your work clothes on and start work.' So he had a rig ready, to get the rig ready to go to Kalgoorlie, to go gold exploration drilling. Yeah, so I just walked in there at the right time, so I got the job. I went over there and I was over there for about eight, nine months, drilling for gold and my son Casey come with me. I went to Coffs Harbour for Christmas and he wanted to come back with me. He was only sixteen then, so he came back and he was off-siding for me on the rig.

Yeah, then the work run out there and I came back and … back to Orange. I was sitting around there trying to get a job and I got a job in an orchard; then I was an orchard bloke. So, you know, something a bit different, pruning trees and, you know, like cutting the grass down, slashing the grass down, planting trees and irrigation and all this sort of thing. Putting in new irrigation and digging up old irrigation and, yeah, it was quite interesting, something a bit different.

It was an apple orchard just out of Orange, about fifteen kilometres out of Orange. It was a bit of a change from drilling and working on the cotton, like up in Bourke.[42] And one morning there I got up and I was digging up the old irrigation pipe, and felt a bit crook. So I started to dry retch and I was sweating and I had a cold drink of water and I said, 'Gee, there's something wrong. I'm getting the flu or something.'

Anyway, I started to get pains in the chest and then it sort of dawned on me that I might be having a heart attack. So I jumped in my car and I told the boss I was going into town to see the doctor. So I drove into town. I didn't know I was having a heart attack, but I drove into town for fifteen kilometres and went home [to Joan's] and had a shower and rung the doctor. The doctor said, 'Come straight down.' He put me straight into hospital because I was having a heart attack and I found out this doctor there in the hospital booked me in down to Sydney, to go and have a test done. And they done the test and they found out that the main artery in front of my heart was completely blocked.

So I had to go and have a bypass, but not at that stage actually. I got over that [the first attack] and I went up to Coffs Harbour. It was the second one they sent me to Sydney; the second heart attack I had. That was about twelve months later, or eighteen months after. I come through the first one okay and then I went to work at a place called Bygolly just the other side of Euchareena. They were advertising in the paper for a father and son team with their own caravan. Well, I had Casey and my own caravan so …

This place out at, out past Euchareena, Bygolly station, it was only 6000 acres; it was only a small place. But anyway, it was, you know, sort of fairly rugged country. They advertised there for the father/son team, so I sent up to Case up in Coffs Harbour and asked him if he wanted to come out there with me, so he came down.

I shifted my caravan out there and a couple of days later Casey came down. We were there for about nine months, fencing and yard building and stock work; shearing, crutching, all that sort of stuff. And, yeah, it was good to get back into the stock work after so long. By gee, I tell you, so long away from the

---

42. Bill stayed in his caravan on the orchard through the week and at his sister Joan's in Orange on the weekends.

game and going back on a station like I did in my younger days. Yeah, I was there for about nine months and we were building a sheep yard and a rail fell across my foot and broke a bone in my foot. I went off work there for a long time.

Then I met up with a woman from there, the manager's wife actually, and then I took up with her. Yeah, we ended up getting together, but her husband, he used to treat her pretty badly. One night there he give her a hiding and he broke five of her ribs, so she decided to take off, so she took off down to Bathurst. Casey and I went down there to help her out because she'd just moved into a new place and we went down and laid some lino for her. You know, she bought a bit of furniture and we shifted that in for her and straightened the whole place up, and cleaned it up for her. Yeah, she could hardly get around because of the broken ribs, but he was a real … he was a real mongrel for the way he treated her, 'cause she was a fantastic person.

We stayed together for about, oh gee, eighteen months, two years, I suppose, and she'd got a job in the hospital, I mean, that was her trade. She'd always worked in hospitals and she got a job back there, like taking the meals and that around to the patients and working in the kitchen. She started there casual, like a couple of days a week, and then she got back on permanent. She got killed going to work. A bloke, a drunk driver, he was going too fast and he come up behind her and run into her and pushed her into the side of a bridge and killed her stone dead. She was a really nice person.

I don't know what that bloke got, but the last I heard he was in Bathurst Gaol. I think he had to come up for court. He was charged with manslaughter.

Driving a Bus in Bathurst

Yeah, and then I went off work so, you know, with this crook foot and I couldn't stand, couldn't walk fast. I was back and forth to the doctor in Sydney and they put me in a calliper. I wear that when my foot gets bad I got to put it on.

And what'd I do then? I drove a bus. I done a course down in Towri in the Aboriginal's thing in Bathurst there. They bought an old convent and they turned it into a place, like for people to come there and college kids going to school, like Aboriginal kids. So they made it into a sort of a hostel for somewhere to live when they were going to school. People come from all over the place, like out around Bourke and Brewarrina and Walgett, all those places, like out bush. And those that wanted to go to the college there, or university in Bathurst, they had somewhere to stay.

So I did a course there driving the bus, looking after the kids like. I was getting paid sort of temporary teachers' wages. I was only doing a few hours a day, like morning and night, but mostly I'd pick up the preschool kids because they used to go there to be helped with their homework. The little kids used to get sent home with homework. Well, their mother and father sort of didn't have time to sit down with them and do it, so they used to go there. They had teachers there at the college, at the Towri, and they used to help the kids, like they'd take them in for a couple of hours and it was my job to pick them up and take them home. So, yeah, it was quite good. It's still going there actually, that thing. It was quite good for the little Aboriginal kids you know to get a chance. They used to go there to get help with their education.[43]

Then I moved back up to Orange and one night there I was watching TV and I had another heart attack and I went into the hospital again. They sent me to Sydney to have the test. So I had the test and found out what had happened. Like, I said before, the main artery in front of my heart was completely blocked. After that heart attack, my daughter, Tracey, she came down with her boyfriend from Coffs Harbour and shifted me up to Coffs Harbour to stay with them.

So I'd moved up there and was waiting to go into hospital. While I was waiting to go into hospital I had another heart attack and that one was really bad. It put me down worse than the other two that I had. And anyway, I was in hospital there for about a fortnight and they shifted me to Sydney by air ambulance to have my operation. I had my operation twelve months ago, just on twelve months ago. Actually another month it'll be twelve months – 18th of next month [January 1994] will be twelve months.

I went back up to Coffs Harbour to get back on my feet again and, well, John was supposed to give me a job there as a security guard in the yard, because he's got trucks there and he's got a big workshop down in Toormina. I was going there. He was going to build a flat up on the top of his building, which he used as a shed, workshop and office. And I was going to live there and just be a security guard, like caretaker, but nothing ever happened. So, yeah, I moved back down to Orange then, after that, back down to my sister. Now I'm waiting on my compo money to come through, because I'm starting my own business. I'm going to go back out to Bourke and live there and make the authentic boomerangs and see if I can make a living out of that. So I'm looking forward to doing it if I can. Just hopefully it'll take off.

---

43. Towri was the former All Hallows Convent School run by the Dominican sisters. It was given to the Bathurst Aboriginal community in 1984 and renamed Towri Aboriginal Corporation. During the 1990s it was a hostel for Aboriginal Students attending Charles Sturt University. In 2005 it was leased to the Bathurst Christian School.

Having a Go – Discrimination – Acceptance

But one thing I would like to say about my people, and I don't want to put them down ... I'm no saint, but I had enough guts to get up and have a go, I suppose, which'd only be the truth. And I know it's pretty hard, I know it's very hard for the people all over Australia – like the Aboriginal people – they don't get much of a go, but they got to be prepared when they get the chance to get out and have a go. If you don't try you never succeed and I think that's one thing that everybody's got to realise, you know, with the Mabo thing and all that that's going on. But if anybody ever hears this tape my advice'd be to them that if they try and improve themselves, they've got to be prepared to get out and have a go.

Yeah, seeing it's starting to get to the end of the interview ... All my life, I mean, there is one issue I want to talk about, and that is about racism in Australia, like how many times I came up against it. Well, I have come up against it quite a few times. The first time, actually, was in Bourke. I walked in the pub – I never drank – and I walked in the pub with my uncle and he was sort of pretty fair. Well, you wouldn't know he was a blackfella. But anyway, we walked in the pub and the publican said, 'Well, I'll serve you, 'Ope,' he said, 'but I'm not going to serve him,' meaning me. And Uncle 'Ope said, 'Well, he happens to be my nephew.' So he said, 'If you don't serve me you can stick your pub,' and we walked out. And that's how it used to be in Bourke. Not only me, I mean, it happened to a lot of other people as well.

And the second time I come across it was [when] I got sent up to a place just out of Roma in Queensland when I was working for Dick Adams at Narran and

Wingadee. He had a mob of sheep he'd bought in shares with his mate. It was a mob of ewes, 1000 ewes. So anyway, he sent me up there to help with the lamb marking. There was me and my little brother Barry Hogan, well, he's not my brother, but we were reared up together. Anyway, we went up there to help out with the lamb marking. One day I walked into the pub because it was pretty hot. I was wearing a cocky's hat and shorts, long socks and shoes and had a tie, and walked into the pub, and I was standing there and, you know, I was wondering why they wouldn't serve me. Anyway, I said, 'Excuse me,' and the girl come up and said, 'Well, I'm sorry, I can't serve you 'cause we don't serve Aboriginals in this pub.' So I said, 'Well, thanks very much,' and just walked out.

The other time it happened was in Dubbo when I was going with Val, the woman that had all my children. We had a friend, a friend of ours, the bloke was in the Vietnam War and he was a sergeant and he was in full uniform. He was going with Joyce, this friend of Val's.

Anyway, we were going out on the town, so we went to this hotel first, in Dubbo. It just so happened it was my shout so I walked up and everybody was dressed for the occasion. The girls were dressed nice and I had a suit on, a tie, and Jack was in his full uniform. And anyway, it was my shout and I walked up to the little servery between the lounge and the public bar. This barmaid was there and I'm waiting and waiting and I said, like, 'Excuse me, can I get a jug of beer,' and she had tears in her eyes, this poor barmaid. You know, I think she was a bit embarrassed about not serving me.

But the bloke that owned the pub, he was an ex-copper and I think he done a lot of time out around Brewarrina somewhere; out west, anyway. He said, 'We don't serve blackfellas in this pub,' so anyway, Jack got very, very annoyed and he was going to let the bloke have it. Of course Val started to cry and the women got upset. Everybody got upset bar myself. But after I thought about it, I mean, it was, you know, a bit of a shock and it hurt me a bit, but it didn't worry me that much because I'd run into it before. But I thought it was pretty tough, like a big place like Dubbo. I mean, it didn't matter. The way I thought of it was, well they're judging me by my colour just because I was black and I thought that was pretty weak. They didn't know me from a bar of soap. They didn't know what sort of person I was, but just because I had black skin I wasn't allowed to have the beer. That was in the sort of late '60s but it still goes on. It's still going on today. I can sympathise with a lot of these … with a lot of these blackfellas, you know, when they get knocked back like that. I can imagine the way they feel, like all these big riots that go on. In this day and age it shouldn't happen. We should be living together and being Australians; yeah, not black and white. We should be all Australians and work together and help one another, but I can imagine how they feel.

I just wonder to myself, you know, like back before I was born, like my people, the things that they had to put up with. I've heard stories about them working on properties and being fed at the wood heap and … well, even me and my old uncle, like all the work we done for cockies from Enngonia right through to Weilmoringle and Brooksville and Glenora and Widgee Downs and Dunsandle. Now, Dunsandle was a place that if ever you went through there the boss, old Harry Conroy, no matter what time of the day it was, you always got a meal, but you always sat out the back of the house at a little table, you know, the blackfellas.

But I mean he was a good old bloke. It was probably the way he was brought up, I don't know. But we always thought he was a great old bloke because any time of the day, if it was 10 o'clock in the morning, if it was 5 o'clock in the afternoon, you still had to go to the house to have a meal. And he'd say, 'Oh, you'd better go up to the house,' he said, 'the missus 'll cook you something,' you know, give you something to eat. And we always sat out the back, never missed, and we done a lot of work for him, too, fencing and that.

Yeah, getting back to the – like having a meal at any station – back in those days, out west, you were always put out the back of the house at a table on the back verandah, or at the back door. And when I first went to New Park over the border … when I worked for old Alec Cuffe. When I first went there, old Bertie Powell and myself, we used to have our meals on the back verandah. Sometimes, especially in the summer, old Alec and his wife used to come out and eat with us. But never ever took us inside.

Towards the end of my time there, just before I got married to Joanie McCarthy, I was there by myself, I went up one morning, I looked at the back table and there was no plates set there and no knife and fork like, when you usually went in for your breakfast, and I thought, 'Gee, what's going on here?'

as though they mightn't be going to feed me or something. Anyway, I went and sat down there and waited and Alec Cuffe come out and he said, 'Bill, you'll be eating with us from now on.' So I went inside in the kitchen. It was getting cold then, too, and he had the big fire going there and I thought how warm it was, being in the kitchen. So, anyway, I started eating with them and, you know, the main meal at tea time, well, we ate in the lounge and I was just like one of them. They sort of started treating me like a human being.

Well, as far as I was concerned I was no better than anybody else, but yeah, they were the first people that ever took me inside. Then after that another bloke I used to work for, Hughie Balcombe … I hadn't seen Hughie Balcombe and his wife since his girls were small. Like, I was only sixteen when I left there and I hadn't seen Hughie Balcombe for years and years and years. And when I came to Orange I found out that he'd bought a place just out of Orange.

What he used to do after he sold his properties, like out around Enngonia, he used to buy these old houses because he was a carpenter by trade, and he used to buy these old houses, do them up and then sell them for a profit. As far as I know he's still doing that today. But anyway, this time I found out that he was living around Orange, so I started making inquiries and I found out where he was living. Now, all the time I worked there at Ellerslie, I used to always have my meals out the back on the little table where the telephone was, just in the back door. I used to always eat there. Anyway, it surprised me – I mean, I'm a man sort of in my forties then when I saw him again and I was only a kid when I left there [Ellerslie].

And Mrs Balcombe, Hughie's wife, she came out and threw her arms around me and kissed me on the cheek, yeah, and I was very surprised at that. I said [to myself], 'Gee whizz, these people have changed or something,' because, I mean, back in those days, I mean the boss's wife would never kiss a blackfella on the cheek. You know, that was a no-no. But then it happened to me and I was very surprised and they said, 'Come in, come in.' They were so glad to see me. And anyway, their daughter turned up and Diane was sort of like five year old and she was sort of in her thirties then and pregnant, you know, and she come in and she said, 'Oh, my old mate', she said and yeah, it was good.

PART FOUR

An awful lot's happened since then

– Jim Kiley

Beyond Oodnadatta – Desert People

It's pretty hard to think of everything. So I'll go back to something I meant to mention earlier. This first story's about when I worked at Narran, just out of Charleville. This Dick Adams, he owned a place in shares with a bloke, Mr Walker, up in South Australia, just out from Oodnadatta, a place called Everard Park.

He used to go up there for the cattle muster. Dick Adams used to go from [inaudible]. He had two places there, Narran and Winkleigh, and I was on Narran. But we used to work the both places together. They were about fifteen mile apart, I suppose. And anyway, I pestered Dick Adams to go out to Everard Park for the muster because I wanted to go to learn from the Aboriginal ringers there on the station.[44] Like, I mean they were smart men with cattle and I thought that they could learn me a few things so I pestered him.

Anyway, he took me and we went up there and I was staying in the house with Dick, Walker and his wife, and a few other people that worked on the place. The homestead had a big high fence around it and it also had single quarters there and, you know, the main house, but everybody'd eat in the main house. We all ate together. It was a great experience, because these men were very good ringers. Like those paddocks up there are big; Everard Park was a big place. I forget how big it was, but it was a big place [about 28,000 square miles in area] and they only ran cattle there. It was all cattle country. And these Aboriginal

---

44. Ringer is a common outback term for a stockman.

ringers used to go out and bring in the mobs of cattle.[45] When a bullock'd break these fellows would sort of step off a horse at flat gallop and just tail a bullock over, and then the other bloke'd be right there with the hobbles[46] to put on him. It's just the way they did it. I mean, they did it every day of their lives. It was just done real easy like. They just used horse hobbles, same as you put on a horse, yeah.

And another thing that happened there on the place, they wanted to initiate me to the tribe because I was black. This Danny, the bloke that would look after the garden and look after the lawn and things like that, and he told me about it. He said, 'You want to watch out,' he said, 'the old fellas are going to get you and initiate you into the tribe.' So I started packing and was ready to leave. The first plane came in – I was gone!

But before that, this King Everard … Mrs Walker used to get all these second-hand clothes, like most of it from St Vincent de Paul and the Salvation Army, and she'd sort of get bundles there when she'd go into town and bring it back and distribute it through the camp. And King Everard, he had a red jumper and a yellow jumper. And he had the red jumper on, like he put it over his body. And anyway, he tied the yellow one around the front, and it was just hanging down the front and no one knew.

Yeah, it was like an apron, 'cause they were pretty primitive. I mean, a lot of the … you know, the kids there would run around with no clothes on. Anyway, they used to come up on a Friday to get their rations and this King Everard came up and Mrs Walker took the little box out with his tobacco and tea and sugar and stuff like that and, anyway, he took his stuff at the gate and then when he turned around he had his bare backside showing. There was nothing on behind, you know, and he had no trousers on, see. He just had the piece tied across the front. But Dick Adams and I were sitting on the verandah and we just had to laugh. It was a classic.

---

45. Probably Jangkuntjara people.
46. Hobbles are used to stop stock, usually horses, from straying too far from the drover's camp, town common or homestead. They consist of two leather straps located around each lower front leg and joined together by another strap or chain. While the animal can feed and roam freely, its ability to travel far, or fast, is minimised.

Memorable Anecdotes

Yeah, another story there, going back to when we worked – old Uncle Alf and I and Walter Thompson – we'd worked on different places along there from Enngonia out towards Weilmoringle. This one place we were on, because they couldn't keep the cattle separated, they'd just sort of roam from Brooksville to Glenora. And Ken Stulley owned Brooksville and Alan White owned Glenora and … 'cause when the muster came all the cattle had to be mustered together. So we had to sort them out, we had to draft them to find out who owned what, see. The cattle'd just knock the fences down and wander backward and forwards.

So anyway, we were sitting around having smoko or having dinner, and Walter Thompson was with us, of course, and old Micky Collis was with us. There was Ernie White, old Alan's son, and young Allan junior, Ken Stulley and Tom Stulley, Uncle Alf and myself. We were all sitting around having dinner and of course old Alan White used to bring the cookie tin, you know, like in the tuckerbox. And he walked around and offered to everybody like, 'Would you like a cake?' or a biscuit or whatever. Anyway, old Walter thought he was going to be sort of above everybody else, so old Mr White said, 'Walter, would you like another cookie?' and he said, 'No, thanks, Mr White,' he said, 'elephant went fishing.' Instead of 'elegant sufficiency', he said, 'Elephant went fishing.' He thought that was close enough.

Yeah, another story, old Uncle Alf told me once about up at Nockatunga. If the white blokes ran in around the young girls, the old blokes used to get them and fix them up, and if there was a, you know, somebody in the tribe that was bad blood – like fighting and drinking, all this sort of stuff – they didn't want to breed from him, so the old people used to whistlecock them.[47] And when they did that it was a matter of nicking them in the right spot. 'Cause then they couldn't stand up and have a pee like a man They'd have to sit down like a woman. Yeah, urinate sitting down like a woman, yeah. It was very strange.

Another thing, too, I should have said earlier was when I came back on one of my trips from overseas I took my boys on a camping trip up to Tibooburra. We bought a metal detector and went up there for a week or so. And my old mate, old Ray Gordon, he came with us. We lived out on the goldfields there and we found some water there. Anywhere in that country, if you're at the right place, you'd find a soak and if you dug down a couple of foot you'd always get beautiful water. So the people, the white people, were saying, 'How come you don't go into town to cart your water?' And because we knew where it was we had no reason to go into town. It was the middle of summer. It was hot and we had two soaks: we had one for the cooking and one for having a bogie, a bath in, yeah.

There is another story there about a snake. We was working on Ellerslie and the old uncle drove the Land Rover in the shed this day and he stepped out of the Land Rover and stepped on this snake's tail. The snake came straight back up over and old uncle threw himself against the car and the snake hit the ground alongside of him. He had a few goes at him, that snake. Another time he [Alf] was in the [pit] toilet and he rolled up the newspaper and the snake flattened his head. He was at the door and he rolled up the newspaper and he was singing out to me. I was over in the kitchen in the shearers' quarters and he was hitting the snake with the rolled up paper, newspaper. I come flying over and, I don't know, but this snake had a set on old Uncle Alf for some reason.

And another time the sheep rushed in the yard and knocked the yard over. We were putting the posts back in and putting the rails up and this snake came across the yard, so we chased him again and he bailed up again and old uncle said, 'Well, look', he said, 'we gotta get this snake because he's gonna end up

---

47. Whistlecock refers to the Aboriginal practice of slitting the urethra on the underside of the penis, preventing semen from entering the sexual partner. It was performed on those whom the elders considered unsuitable for reproduction, for whatever reason.

getting one of us.' So the snake used to live down the lavatory hole. And so we backed the truck up near the thing and I lay in the back and waited.

We put the truck sort of fairly close and we was laying in the back of the truck. We used to take it in turns. But the snake used to just put his head up and look around, then he'd go back down again. Anyway, it so happened that I was the one that got him. He came out a bit and I ended up fluking him. I shot him.

Yes, we'll go back to South America there. I was sitting in a bar one night, having a cold beer and this poor guy walked in and he'd just done a day's work and I think he got paid about 30 sucres, which is about a buck, and he had a wife and three or four kids. He was buying some rations to take home like rice and salt and stuff like that. I started talking to the guy and I bought him a beer and I started to ask him about what sort of work he had and what wages he was getting and he told me and I said, 'Well, gee whiz, you can't feed four kids on that,' because it was only a little lunch bag sort of thing, of rice. It wasn't even full, it was only about half full, probably about a big handful I'd say.

So anyway I bought him some. I got tinned meat and rice and salt and coffee and bought him a fair bit of stuff and this bloke couldn't thank me enough. As a matter of fact, he got hold of my hand and he didn't want to let it go. Anyway, he went out of there sort of half stunned. I bought him a couple of beers and he took the stuff home to his family. Eggs and everything, I bought him, but I was so sorry for the poor man. I mean, they worked really hard.

Yes, just one thing about old Uncle Alf's young boy, Barry. He was the only boy, there was three girls and a boy and he was second eldest. And he wrote me a letter when he was sixteen and I could hardly understand it, but I could make out a part where he said, 'Come and pick me up at Brewarrina,' and I was working at Narran out of Charleville. Anyway I jumped in my car and came down to Bourke and across to Brewarrina and picked him up and took him with me, because we used to be pretty close.

Anyway, he knew that I was married to Darby McCarthy's sister and being a little jockey-sized fella, he wanted to go into the stables. So he came up to Narran and the boss gave him a job there and, actually, I taught him to ride a horse. Anyway, we went to Brisbane and I spoke to Darby about it and Darby said, 'Yes,' he would see what he could do. So he did get him into a stable in

Brisbane and Barry started strapping and trackwork and that. Then he went to work for a bloke in Gympie, who was the mayor of Gympie, and towards the end of his career he won two jockey premierships; he won two in a row. He sent me clippings and that of all the horses in the races he'd won, mostly country races, but, yes, he went on to win a fair few big country races. Then he got kicked and it nearly killed him. He got kicked by a horse and they had to take half his lung away because his ribs went through his lung, punctured his lung. Yes, he nearly died, but anyway he had to get out of it [the game].

He now works for Grascos. Yes, wool rolling and piece picking. He works all around Brewarrina, Bourke, but now I think he's down in Dubbo, because he mostly lives with Tommy Gordon, which was one of the people that reared him up when his mother and father died; he went with old Bertie and Edi Gordon. And Tommy usually lives with Bert's son

Family Secrets

Yes, earlier I said where Mum had died of suspicious circumstances. Well, there was an inquest held in Bourke – I'm nearly sure it was Bourke – but no one would come forth and give evidence. And her stepfather was sort of blamed, but no one would say.

His name was George Knight. I found out only about six weeks ago. I always thought that I was George Gray's son, because he's my father on my birth certificate, but I found out from Auntie Betty, Betty Ebsworth, Ngaka Ebsworth's wife. I was always suspicious because there was some things in my life that didn't add up. So I knew that Auntie Betty would probably be the last one to tell me because she was the oldest Knight left and all the others had passed on. And I asked her and I said, 'Well, would you tell me the truth?' because people had only hinted at it before that. And she said, 'Yes, if I can I will.' So I said, 'Who was my father?' And she told me who it was and it was George Knight, not George Gray. So all the years, and even through this interview, I always said he was my grandfather; and Uncle 'Ope, he was my stepbrother.

And the same with Alf Hagen's wife. She was Janet Knight and I always thought that she was … I was always brought up to call her Auntie Janet, but she was my stepsister. And living, you know, like, with all those people, in all those years, that no one would ever say anything about her. All I could think of – I mean, I'm pleased to know who my real father was, even though he's dead and gone, because he died back in about '48, '49. And Opie Knight must have known, but he never ever told me, even though we were pretty close. And being close, as we were, I think he sort of knew that I was his half-brother. Then I went back to Bourke only a few weeks ago and told some people and they said, 'We already knew that.' But my sister and myself were the last ones to find out. He fathered both of us to his step-daughter.

Like Opie Knight, Janet Knight and Jean Knight, who was my mother, they all had the same mother, but a different father. George Knight fathered Opie and Janet Knight, and he fathered Joanie and I to his stepdaughter, which is a pretty complicated thing. But back in those days, no one was allowed to talk about it because the old people would always say, 'Well, you're putting them down,' you know, by saying that, and I think that's why they sort of hushed it up.

June's father was – what was his name? – Martin, Gunyen Martin. Yes, he was June's father.

About my mother's death, well, what I heard … I just know what people told me. Like, Janet Knight told me that she was poisoned with strychnine and they said it was suicide. And when the inquest was held … I mean, when the court case was over, they put it down as suicide, but there was suspicious circumstances and they thought that he might have done it himself, like, George Knight, because he was jealous of her. I mean, it's not for me to say and I'm not ashamed to say that he is my dad, because it was just a relief to find out the truth, but I always knew there was something suspicious and I always knew there was something that people were holding back and would never come out and say, when I asked for the truth.

Auntie Betty told me a couple of other people that might be able to tell me a bit more. She came up from Sydney, she used to live in Sydney. And she came up to Bourke when she was in her teens and she met Ngaka Ebsworth and she didn't want to go back to Sydney. She wanted to stay there with Ngaka, but she was only about fifteen or sixteen; she was only a girl herself. But, see, she never knew. I asked her who my mother's father was and she couldn't tell me. She couldn't even tell me who her mother was because she lived away, you see, she lived in Sydney. But she said I might be able to find out from Eileen Hunt, who was a Leppett, Eileen Leppett. Her mother was a Knight, which was Eva Knight, but she has passed on too. See, she would be about the oldest.

There is her and Evelyn Crawford that knew Mum and they're about the

Auntie Evelyn Crawford and Billy at Evelyn's place in Brewarrina, 1998.

oldest living and the only ones probably that could tell me whose Mum's father and mother was, 'cause I never knew.[48] And I mean, all the people are dead, like Opie Knight – one that I could have asked, but he's dead – and Janet Knight, she's dead. All the old people are just about finished, you know, all the Knights. There's only just the kids left and nobody can tell me anything, but anyway, I've got to find out and I've got to go back to the court case and see if I can get a copy of the inquest and read it for myself, just to find out a bit more.

---

48. In 1994 Evelyn Crawford told Chris Woodland that when he saw Billy or Joanie Gray next to tell them to see her as she 'had something that wasn't hers to keep'. That was her poetic way to say that she had knowledge that should be passed onto Billy and Joan. Several months later Chris took Billy over to Brewarrina from Bourke for the day and left Billy in Evelyn's company for a couple of hours. Evelyn told Billy that she was there at the reserve on the bank of the Darling at Bourke when his mother died. She was carrying buckets of water from the river when she collapsed, dying later. Evelyn Crawford's fascinating book *Over My Tracks: A Remarkable Life*, as told to Chris Walsh, was published in1993 by Penguin Books Australia Ltd.

Bush Tucker and Leaf Players

Yes, going back to the early part where old Uncle Alf, like, reared me up when Mum died and he taught me everything I knew. In the bush he used to point out different bushes and the different trees in the bush about … like one was the emu bush and he always said that if you found a few of them on the red country, or on the black country – very seldom you see them on the black country – but where you found them, if there was a few of them, there was shallow bore water or well water, probably at 30, 40 feet. And it was always beautiful water; very soft water.

The other things he told me about was the gargaloos; we used to call them gargaloos, but they're sort of a wild banana or bush banana or bush pear, whatever you liked to call them, but we've always known them as gargaloos and we used to cook them in the ashes and eat them.[49] And the other one was a wild potato – we'd call them potato and we used to cook that in the ash as well. There is a few others – I forget – well, quandong's another one, but I mean, everybody used to eat them. I mean, they're sort of scattered. A funny thing, you know, in Western Australia when I was working over in Kalgoorlie – I came back over to Norseman, I done a contract in Norseman – and you know along the highways there, you always find quandongs. There's quandong trees along the road there and they grow all the year round over there.

Over round here, like New South Wales and out around Enngonia, there's

---

49. Gargaloo (*Parsonsia eucalyptophylla*) is a vigorous vine that grows along the ground or over living or dead trees.

only one time of the year that you find the fruit. Yes, but I was quite shocked, actually, because to find these, like quandongs in that time of the year in Western Australia, it was a bit hard to believe but they're there. They were growing and I ate them, and I knew they were quandongs.

The only thing now with the quandong, you get a lot of grubs, you know, you've got to be careful when you pick them. You've got to break them open because they get a lot of grubs in them. Years ago we used to make jam out of them; make pies out of them, but the jam was beautiful. I can remember old Alan White on Glenora. We were going through there once up to Brooksville and old Alan White never drank, and neither did my old uncle. Anyway, old Alan White made some wine out of the quandongs and I can remember sitting in the back of the old Chev and he said to old Uncle Alf, he said, 'Well, Alf, you don't drink and I don't drink, so we'll have a drink,' and they had a sip of this quandong wine that he'd made and his wife used to make the jam. Yes, I remember that. The way he came out with it, 'You don't drink and I don't drink,' he said, 'so we'll have a drink.'

Old Billy Reid was a leaf player, of course. And old Alf Edwards used to play the leaf. Old Ray Gordon used to play the leaf. But come to think of it … now, it comes to mind that I can remember Cliffy and Morris playing the leaf at Enngonia. That was Alf Edwards' younger brothers, old Alf Edwards' younger brothers, Cliffy and Morris Edwards. I think Morris lives in Dareton now and I think Cliffy is in Bathurst, but I'm not too sure about that. But come to think of it, it just came to mind that they did. I can remember them playing the leaf, yes.

I want to thank you for having me do this because we put it off for about – if I can remember rightly, about three or four years. We have been wanting to do this for a long time and I want to thank you and your wife, Virginia, and all the other people that I met [in] coming to Canberra, and look forward to doing it again, mate.

Postscript

For the last few years of his life Billy lived at Tamworth. Two of his boys were living and working with him at Bourke and he thought that Tamworth would offer them better opportunities and, he thought, less disturbing influences on lads of their impressionable years. Of course Bourke was always Billy's spiritual home, but he welcomed the new life at Tamworth, particularly as he was now living at the centre of his beloved country music.

As the years wore on his health kept deteriorating. He had always been active and had enjoyed a strong work ethic but diabetes and a worsening heart condition slowly made him less mobile and less involved with the community.

My family, from the South Coast, Canberra and Sydney, visited our old friend in September 2010 and enjoyed a reunion with Billy and some of his family.

Billy was rushed to the Tamworth Base Hospital on Sunday night, 15 May 2011, with kidney failure and was placed on oxygen. I was notified the following day and spoke to him that evening on the phone. As he was on oxygen I was surprised that I was permitted to speak to him, but I am so pleased I could. His last few words to me were filtered by the oxygen mask, but were easily understood. He told me that he had had enough. He died at 4.30 am the following morning, 17 May. In general terms, Billy's death certificate states that he died of cardiac and kidney failure.

The funeral and wake for Billy were held on 23 May and were attended by family members and friends from as far afield as Mildura, Broken Hill, Coffs

Harbour, Dubbo, Canberra, the NSW South Coast and, of course, Bourke. I was privileged to write and deliver his eulogy.

Billy's ashes were returned to Bourke. His grave and his mother's adjoin each other. Billy's headstone in the Bourke cemetery bears the following inscription:

> William James Gray
> 'Bill'
> 15/6/1940 – 17/5/2011
> Beloved Father Of
> Tracy, Casey, Valissa, Justin,
> Megan, Clayton
> Brother Of Joan & June
> Father-in-Law, Grandfather &
> Great Grandfather Of Their Families

Billy with his grand-daughters, Kiara, Jacinta, Brooke and Stacey.

Billy with granddaughter Stacey, Kelly Woodland, son Tracey, son Justin, Virginia Woodland, Sean Woodland and Col Gee, September 2010.

Justin Gray and children, Jacinta and Jackson, Tamworth, May 2011

Family at Billy's wake, Tamworth, May 2011. L to R: David, Valissa, Megan, Tracey, Justin, Val Grant (mother of Billy's children.), Clayton and Casey.

Old Mates. Col, Billy and Chris, Tamworth, September 2010.

Billy's sister Joan Kelly (nee Gray) at her brother's wake. The two were very close.

The last farewell. Billy and Chris Woodland at Billy's home in Tamworth. Though always in touch with each other this was to be their last meeting, 3 September 2010.

Index

Adams, Dick, 146, 150, 151
Adelaide Street, Bourke NSW, 27, 31
Adelaide, SA, 107
Afghans, 26
Albury, NSW, 136, 138
Anderson, Johnny, 86
Andy, Ike, 62, 63
Araluen, NSW, 67, 69
Arjune (Afghan), 26
Asamera Oil (Indonesia) Ltd, 127
Austral Street, Kempsey NSW, 9
Australian Hotel, Bourke, 78

Balcombe, Bill, 34
Balcombe, Diane, 149
Balcombe, Hughie 34, 149
Balcombe, Mrs, 149
Balts, 76, 77
Barcoo rot, 23
Barringun, NSW, 72
Bates, Bert, 76
Bathurst, NSW, 143, 144, 160
Beechworth, Vic, 137
Bendigo, Vic, 93
Billingham, David, 13
Bismarck, 56–57
Bjelke-Peterson, Joh, 87, 88
Bobadah, NSW, 25
Bogota, Columbia, 102, 120
Booth, Tommy, 21
Boulia, Qld, 85
Boyd, Vic, 102
Bradley, Kevin, 14
Breeza Plains, NSW, 95
Brisbane 90–93, 154–155
Brewarrina, NSW, 16, 33, 42, 43, 50, 68, 144, 147, 154, 155
Broken Hill, NSW, 161
Brooksville station, 25, 30–34, 51, 65, 66, 68, 148, 152, 160
Brown, Euley, 53, 64
Burnt Bridge, Kempsey NSW, 9
Bygolly station, 142

Calabozo, Venezuela, 120
Calgary, Canada, 103
Campbell, Robin 'Quartpot', 74
Canberra ACT, 126, 135, 160, 161
Caqueta, Venezuela, 120–122
Caracas, Venezuela, 120, 122, 123
Carnarvon Gorge/Range, 71, 74
Carroll, Tom, 9
Cartagena, Colombia, 119, 120
Charleville, Qld, 84, 150, 154
Chiltern, Vic, 137
Chinaman, Georgie, 20, 22
Chipparro, 115, 116
Chone, South America, 105–110, 112, 114, 131
Clyde Cameron College, Wodonga Vic, 136
Coffs Harbour, NSW, 126, 141, 142, 145, 161
Colebaggy Creek, NSW, 95
Collis, Micky, 152
Colombia, South America, 103, 111–121

Connellan, Mickey, 88, 89
Conroy, Harry, 43, 148
Coolac, NSW, 137
Cooper(s) Creek, Qld, SA, 23
Corowa, NSW, 137
Cox, Charlie, 40
Cox, Ted (Detective), 80
Cranfield, Mark, 14
Crawford, Evelyn, 157
Crystal, David, 11
Cuffe, Alec, 41, 71, 73, 78, 79, 82, 148, 149
Cuffe, George, 82
Cuffe, Joy (Mrs), 71, 73, 75, 78, 81
Culgoa River, NSW, 136
Cullen, Clive, 16, 24
Cullen, Maisie, 16, 24
Cullen, Margaret, 16, 24
Cullen, Mickie, 24
Cummin, Darcy, 84, 85, 86, 87, 88, 89
Cunnamulla, Qld, 7, 33, 40, 55, 57, 58, 64, 70, 73, 74, 75, 78, 83

Dakota Drillers, 137
Dareton, NSW, 160
Darwin, NT, 9
Davis Jr, Sammy, 76
Delhi, India, 129, 135
Diamantina River, Qld, 85, 86
DMR (Department of Main Roads, NSW), 15, 16, 78
Doll Doll, *see* Marinor
Duaringa, Qld, 87
Dubbo, NSW, 52, 94, 97, 100, 102, 121, 125, 129, 135, 136, 138, 147, 155, 162
Dunsandle station, 43, 148
Dutton, Trevor, 62

Ebsworth, Betty, 27, 30
Ebsworth, Ngaka, 27, 156
Echuca, Vic, 93
Ecuador, South America, 101, 103, 104, 105, 107, 112, 113, 114, 117, 120
Edungalba, Qld, 87, 87, 88
Edwards, Alf, 31, 62, 160
Edwards, Alice, 31, 60, 64
Edwards, Charlie, 32
Edwards, Cliff, 62, 160
Edwards, Dawn, 32, 62
Edwards, Lyle, 31
Edwards, Maurice, 62, 160
Edwards, Pierce, 32
Ellerslie station, 30, 31, 34, 36, 40, 43, 66, 149
Ellwood, Ernie 'Cook', 19, 79
Enngonia, NSW, 28, 30, 31, 34, 39, 41, 59, 60, 61, 64, 65, 66, 70, 73,75, 76, 78, 149, 152, 153, 159
Eucharina, NSW, 142
Eulo family, 53, 62, 64, 70
Eumungerie, NSW, 94, 95, 138
Evans, Jim, 94
Everard Park station, SA, 150

Federal Hotel/Motel, Bourke, 77
Fords Bridge, NSW, 34, 47

166

Franklin, Sambo, 76, 77

Gables, The, Bourke, 28, 31, 78
Gardner, Alan, 60
Gardner, Roy, 60
Gargaloo (bush banana), 159
Gatum Gatum (racehorse), 84, 86
Gee, Colin, 32, 62, 78, 163, 164
Gilbert, 25
Gilgandra, NSW, 94, 136, 137
Gillon, Noel, 55
Glenora station, 34, 66, 148, 152, 160
Goodooga, NSW, 33
Goodwin, Ray, 107
Gordon, Bertie, 155
Gordon, Digger, 36,
Gordon, Edi, 155
Gordon, Mrs, 68
Gordon, Ray, 34, 36, 40, 41, 67, 153, 160
Gordon, Stella, 67, 68
Gordon, Tommy, 155
Grant, Kenny, 136
Grant, Shelley, 14
Grant, Valerie/Val, 94, 97, 98, 100, 125, 147
Gray, Barry, 139
Gray, Casey, 125, 141, 142, 143, 164
Gray, Clayton, 98, 125, 164
Gray, David, 98, 125, 164
Gray, George, 15, 18, 24, 28, 156
Gray, Gina, 97, 98, 125
Gray, Joan (Joanie), 13, 17, 18, 20, 23–25, 28, 29, 31–33, 41, 51, 62, 65, 140, 142, 157, 165
Gray, June (Junie), 18, 20, 24, 29, 31, 41, 157
Gray, Justin, 13, 125, 163, 164
Gray, Megan, 125, 164
Gray, Tracey, 125, 145, 164
Gray, Velecia, 125
Guayaquil, Ecuador, 104, 106, 114
Gundagai, NSW, 137
Gunger One, *see* Moreen
Gypsies, 26

Hagan, Albert, 54
Hagan, Alf, 10, 16, 18, 20, 24–26, 28, 30, 33, 34, 37, 39, 42, 45,46,54, 56, 57, 65, 66, 152–154, 156, 159, 160
Hagan, Barry, 41, 154
Hagan, Bobby, 57
Hagan, Daphne, 41
Hagan, Dawn, 41
Hagan, Dorothy, 41
Hagan, Freddy, 57
Hagan, Jimmy, 54
Hagan, Stephen, 14
Hall, Ben (bushranger), 51
Hammersley Ranges, WA, 96
Hart, Bumpety, 64
Hart, George, 64
Hill, Andrew, 20
Hodge, Gidgee, 52
Hodge, Mrs, 52
Hogan, Barry, 147
Honolulu, Hawaii, USA, 102, 103
Hooper, Doreen, 78
Hooper, Roger, 59, 60
Howard, Bob, 55
Howie, Keith, 28
Howlett, Billy, 16, 33, 35, 36
Hubbard, Bob, 23
Hull Fred, 20, 51
Hunt/Leppett, Eileen, 157
Huston, USA, 98, 102, 121, 123, 125
Hyles, Harry, 88, 89

Indonesia, 10, 127–130, 132, 133

Jackson, Shilling, 74
Johnson, Amy, 16
Johnson, Duck 16, 18, 23
Johnson, Lennie 'Norto' 48, 52
Johnson, Ruby, 18
Johnson, Stephie, 52

Kalgoorlie, WA, 141, 143, 159
Kelly, Betty 'Googie', 60
Kempsey, NSW, 9
Kenny, Cecil, 34
Kiley, Jim, 13
Kilgour, Ted, 60, 66
King Everard, 151
King Wally, 49
Kirby, Evelyn, 78
Knight, Albert, 18, 54
Knight, Archie, Jr, 59, 66
Knight, Archie, Sr, 18, 19, 26, 54, 55, 76
Knight, Betty, 27, 157
Knight, Eva (Granny Evie), 62, 157
Knight family, 40
Knight, George, 20, 21, 51, 156, 157
Knight, Harry, 26
Knight, Hope Alexander (Opie), 18, 46, 55, 62, 63, 76, 77, 135,146,156, 157, 158
Knight, Janet, 16, 18, 20, 26, 28, 33, 40, 156–158
Knight, Nelly, Granny, 47, 49
Knight, Nita, 46
Knight, Yvonne, 55, 56, 140

Lake Mere (Toorale station), 29, 37
Lake Nash, NT, 71, 74
Leek, Ray 92
Leppett, *see* Hunt
Little, Jimmy (singer), 68
Lloyd, Ted, 79
Longreach, Qld, 84
Los Angeles, USA, 102
Louth, NSW, 18, 55
Lucas, Baker, 57

Mackie, Jeanie, 27
Madagascar, 92
Manta, Ecuador, 110, 112
Maps, 2, 3
Maracaibo, Colombia, 119, 120, 123
Marinor, Charlie (Doll Doll), 18, 19
Martin, Gunyen, 157
Martin, Harry, 33
Mays Bend, North Bourke, 76
McCarthy, Bertie, 90
McCarthy, Joan (Joanie), 58, 78, 94, 87, 90–92, 148
McCarthy, Richard (Darby), 58, 90, 154
McClelland, Noel, 76
McKellar, Aggie, 16, 18
Melbourne, Vic, 93, 126, 133
Melville Island, NT, 9
Meredith, John, 13
Mildura, Vic, 13, 161
Miles, Qld, 92
Miley, 31
Min light, 43, 44
Mogriguy, NSW, 94, 95, 138
Mooki, NSW, 95
Moonie, Qld, 92
Moreen, 9
Morrel, Murray (Maurie?), 103, 141
Mulwala, NSW, 10
Mumbler family, 9
Mungindi, Jack, 37, 38
Murray River, NSW/Vic, 11
Murray, Stan, 136
Murri, *see* Powell, Bert
Myles, Dieter, 104, 118

Narrabri, NSW, 95
Narran station, 146, 150, 154
Nashville USA, 123
National Library of Australia – Oral History Section, ACT, 11, 12
Native Dog Bore, 34
Nerrigundah, NSW, 67, 68
Netterville, Mike, 116, 120, 122, 123
New Guinea, 92
New Park station, 7, 8 10, 41, 53, 60–68, 70, 72, 75, 78, 82, 148
Ngaka, *see* Ebsworth
Nockatunga station, Qld, 23, 24, 53, 54, 56, 64, 72, 152
Nocoleche station, 54

Nodical, 23
Norseman, WA, 159
North Gregory Hotel, Winton Qld, 85
Nullarbor (Plain), SA, WA, 97, 126
Nunnuttara Roadhouse, WA 98
Nyngan, NSW, 36

O'Lantern/Lantrum, Jack 50, 64, 74
O'Malley family, 65
O'Shannessy, Mick, 141
Oodnadatta, SA, 150,
Orange, NSW, 135, 140–142, 145, 149,
Orcher family, 64,
Orcher, Sonny, 33

Paraburdoo, WA, 96, 98, 99, 102, 125, 126
Perooz, Mrs, 26, 27
Perth, WA, 97–98, 100, 125
Peru, South America, 104
Phillip, Charlie, 46,
Pippos, 32
Piuru, Peru, 105
Police/Copper(s), 9, 16, 18, 25, 26, 31, 48, 49, 55, 60, 61, 74, 79, 80, 84, 86, 147
Potter, Gus, 52
Powell, Bert (Murri), *see also* Murri, 70–74, 148
Puna, Ecuador, 104

Quandong, 160
Quantambone, NSW, 42
Quartpot, *see* Campbell, Robin
Quechua Indians of Ecuador, Bolivia, Chile, 105, 106
Quilpie, Qld, 24, 57
Quirindi, NSW, 125, 136
Quito, Ecuador, 102, 109, 112, 120

Rames, Fred, 79
Randall, Mrs, 21
Rantapunya, 127, 129, 132
Reid, Bill, 160
Reid, Gary, 107, 109
Reynolds, Splinter, 70
Rice, George, 140
Robertson, Frank, 34
Robertson, Malcolm, 34
Rochester, Vic, 93
Rockhampton, Qld, 71, 74, 84–88
Rodriquez, 127, 129, 132
Rolfe, Percy, 47
Roma, Qld, 146
Rowrow, Willy, 87
Royal Hotel, Bourke, 84
Rufus, 22
Rumble, Curly, 45
Rumble, Robbie, 29

Saffey, Bill, 52
Salvation Army, 151
San Antonio, Venezuela, 120, 122
Shillingworth family, 64
Shillingworth, Lyle, 31, 66
Shillingworth, Reggie, 60, 64, 65
Shillingworth, Roy, 31, 64
Shillingworth, Turk, 32, 59, 62, 66
Shovel, George, 35, 40
Siddick, Chrissy, 57, 64
Siddick, Jimmy, 50
Simmons, Pat, 32, 68, 78
Singapore, 125, 127, 129, 132
Slim Dusty, 10
Smith family, 64
Smith, Georgie, 41
Smith, Jimmy, 24, 32
Smith, Percy, 56
Smith, Roy, 31
Snake Bay, Melville Island, NT, 9
Snake Gully, 128
South America, 7, 10, 98, 101, 102, 103, 104, 116, 123, 124, 125, 130, 154
Southwell, Brother, 40, 41
Squeaky Bay, Vic, 93
St George, Qld, 44, 92

St Vincent de Paul, 151
Stulley, Ken, 30
Stulley, Tom, 152
Sullivan family, 64
Sumatra, Indonesia, 128
Surat, Qld, 2
Sydney, NSW, 9, 24, 26, 34, 45, 46, 58, 60, 67, 68, 72, 74, 75, 78, 79, 80, 96, 102, 103, 126, 129, 138, 142, 144, 145, 157, 161

Talbalba station, 31, 66
Tamworth, NSW, 13, 95, 136, 161
Tara, Qld, 91

Taylor family, 51
Thompson, (another) Les, 53
Thompson, Les, 23
Thompson, Walter, 23, 24, 42, 43, 65, 152
Tinapagee station, 54
Tiwi people of Melville and Bathurst Islands, 9
Tom Price, WA, 96
Toorale station, 16, 18, 19, 28, 30, 37
Toowoomba, Qld, 58, 91
Tottenham, NSW, 35, 36
Townsville, Qld, 125
Towri Aboriginal Corporation, 13, 144
Troutman, Johnny, 91
Tudor Street, Bourke, 15, 26, 28, 140

United Geophysics, 93

Venezuela, 109, 112, 115–121, 123, 126
Vietnam War, 147

Walgett, NSW, 144
Walker, Mr, 150
Walker, Mrs, 151
Waltara, 40
Wanaaring, NSW, 16, 35, 40, 55
Warella Downs station, 34, 35
Warrego River, 65
Water Commission/Irrigation Commission of NSW, 94
Water Resources of NSW, 94
Watermin Drillers, 135, 136, 141
Wayne, Phil, 93, 94
Wee Waa, NSW, 95
Weilmoringle, NSW, 33, 74, 136, 149, 152
Werris Creek, NSW, 95, 126
Westbeef Pastoral Company, 139
Western Geophysical, 98
Whistlecock, 153
White Rose (café), Cunnamulla, 32
White, Alan Jr, 152, 160
White, Alan Sr, 152
White, Ernie, 152
Widgee Downs station, 31, 66, 148
Widjeri Aboriginal Co-op, Bourke, 55, 140
Willara station, 54
Williams, R.M., 58, 91, 109
Wilson, Benny, 18, 52
Wilsons Promontory, 93
Wingadee, NSW, 147
Winkleigh station, 150
Winton, Qld, 84–86
Wodonga, Vic, 136–138
Woodgell, Angus, 62
Woodland, Chris, 8, 51, 60, 67, 71, 73, 76, 78, 79, 126, 164, 165
Woodland Clan, 13
Woodland, Kelly, 163
Woodland, Kevin, 9
Woodland, Sean, 163
Woodland, Virginia, 13, 160, 163
Wyandra, Qld, 94
Wyong, NSW, 16, 24, 28

Yarrawonga, Vic, 10
York, Barry, 14
Young, Dougie, 57, 58
Young, Robert, 58
Young, Vera, 57

Zane, 115, 116